THE CRUCIFER OF BLOOD

A New Sherlock Holmes Mystery

by

PAUL GIOVANNI

Based on Characters created by
Conan Doyle

Nelson Doubleday, Inc.
Garden City, New York

The original production of *The Crucifer Of Blood* opened at the
Studio Arena Theatre in Buffalo, New York on January 6, 1978.

The Broadway production opened at the Helen Hayes Theatre in
New York City on September 28, 1978. It was presented by
Lester Osterman, Richard Horner, Terry Allen Kramer, and John
Wulp, and directed by Paul Giovanni. Costumes were designed by
Ann Roth, and lighting by Roger Morgan. Scenery was designed
by John Wulp and supervised by Lynn Pecktal.

The Broadway cast, in order of appearance, was as follows:

Major Alistair Ross	Dwight Schultz
Captain Neville St. Claire	Nicolas Surovy
Jonathan Small	Christopher Curry
Durga Dass (A Hindu)	Edward Zang
Wali Dad (An Afghan)	Tuck Milligan
Mohammed Singh (A Mohammedan)	Andrew Davis
Sherlock Holmes	Paxton Whitehead
John Watson, M.D.	Timothy Landfield
Irene St. Claire	Glenn Close
Birdy Johnson	Tuck Milligan
Tonga	Roumel Reaux
Inspector Lestrade	Edward Zang
Fung Tching (A Chinaman)	Melvin Lum
Hopkins (A Policeman)	Martin LaPlatney
Mordecai Smith (A Sailor)	Andrew Davis

SCENE ONE (*Prologue*)
The Red Fort at Agra, India (June, 1857).

SCENE TWO
221-B Baker Street (Thirty years later).

SCENE THREE
(*Part One*) Pondicherry Lodge at Maidenhead (The same day).

(*Part Two*) The same (Two hours later).

SCENE FOUR
The Gate of a Hundred Sorrows, an opium den (The following night).

SCENE FIVE
On the River Thames (Later the same night).

SCENE SIX
221-B Baker Street (Dawn of the next morning).

There is an intermission between scenes three and four.

THE CRUCIFER OF BLOOD

The full material on which this play is based has only recently come to light. It was found among the effects of Dr. John Watson which had passed into the hands of a distant relative, and took the form of a memoir. The first page of that document reads as follows: "The dreadful case of the blood crucifer occurred in London in 1887 and formed one of the most painful and alarming episodes in my long association with Mr. Sherlock Holmes. We were young, and most of our career lay before us. But no event in my subsequent life could ever erase from my mind the pain and horror of the events which it enshrines. If, in future years, some other eye should read this memoir, and some other hand be tempted to present it to the public in narrative form, it will, I hope, become apparent why I myself considered it best to leave unrendered, in the recital of my friend's outstanding cases, the heart of this appalling story.

It had begun, thirty years before, in India, during the Great Mutiny, at the Red Fort of Agra . . ."

Paul Giovanni

SCENE ONE (*Prologue*)

Agra, India. The capital of a district of twenty-five million natives, and a few hundred white men. It is 1857, during the British occupation, in the days of the great Indian mutiny.

The stage is black.

A MUEZZIN howls at the setting sun.

MUESSIN. (*Singing*) Allah ho akabar! ("I proclaim there is no God but God.")

(*Saffron colored light from behind, silhouettes the seventy-fifth gate of the Fort at Agra, India. The gate is an immense open arch with no doors: the ground is paved with Agra stone. It is a quiet evening, shattered, periodically, by the beating of drums, the barking of dogs, and the occasional yell of a jackal.*

TWO HINDUS, *wearing British military uniforms, sit in the gate, stopping their ears against the* MUEZZIN's *Muslim prayer. A young* BRITISH PRIVATE *stands by them holding an Enfield rifle. At the moment these* THREE *are shadows; more of them later. We are looking at the* MEN, *the gate, and the fort from the inside. Through the arch of the gate, on the outside and only a few hundred feet away, the Taj Mahal glimmers in the half light.*

It is very hot.

TWO BRITISH OFFICERS *enter Stage Right.* CAPTAIN NEVILLE ST. CLAIRE *is handsome, rugged and very much a typical English officer and gentleman.* MAJOR ALISTAIR ROSS *is untypical. Cold, effete, and full of questionable humor,* HE *is an odd mixture of malevolence and charm. Both* MEN *are in their twenties.*

ROSS *enters first, reading a large map by the light of a lantern. Pursued by* ST. CLAIRE *who is slightly drunk.* THEY *wear swords at their waists, and pistols in their belts*)

ST. CLAIRE. (*Loud*) Money! Damn you, Ross, I'm talking about money!

ROSS. You lost your temper, St. Claire, at seven this morning, and you haven't got it back yet.

ST. CLAIRE. I need fifty rupees. I need them tonight!

ROSS. Whatever for? You cannot go anywhere.

ST. CLAIRE. Please, Ali. Just fifty. Be a brick!

ROSS. (*Stops and faces him*) Is there a race in the Fort tonight?

ST. CLAIRE. (*Giggles*) At midnight.

ROSS. And where are the horses to run?

ST. CLAIRE. At the square in the old quarter.

ROSS. In six weeks I have barely seen all of the *new* quarter. Besides, there's no map of the old quarter. It's a labyrinth.

ST. CLAIRE. Exactly! But my man showed me how to find the *square*. (Indicating) It's down that way, about a mile or more, past the seven corridors.

ROSS. I find it peculiar, to say the least, that these Indians can so easily arrange a horse race in the middle of a revolutionary uprising.

ST. CLAIRE. There's a superb pony called Tally Dallah. A real flyer!

ROSS. You're such a child, Nelly.

ST. CLAIRE. But I know I can double my money.

ROSS. The only way to double *your* money, dear, is to fold it over once and put it in your pocket.

ST. CLAIRE. But I've seen this pony—

ROSS. (*Cutting him off*) You cannot go off-duty this evening. You and I must watch over twenty-five gates until sunrise.

ST. CLAIRE. Damn this fort! It's as big as England.

ROSS. It was once a great palace. Thousands flocked in and out.

ST. CLAIRE. Let me slip off for an hour, later. You can gate-keep for the both of us.

ROSS. My dear fellow, there's a war on.

ST. CLAIRE. Blast! I know that.

ROSS. Half our sepia army has run off with the weapons we gave them, and now they are coming back to kill us with those very same weapons.

ST. CLAIRE. Those rebels won't come near this fort. Not with Wazir Kahn on the hill.

ROSS. I don't trust Wazir Kahn. He might bolt at any time and join the rebels.

ST. CLAIRE. (*Outraged*) But he's *our* Maharajah!

ROSS. The Maharajah belongs to no one.

ST. CLAIRE. But he does. He belongs to the 37th Battalion. We made him an honorary member and gave him a uniform.

ROSS. Nellie, you are adorable!

ST. CLAIRE. He loves us.

(*A gun shot sounds in the distance.* THEY *are still for a moment*)

Ali, lend me fifty.

ROSS. Why don't you turn yogi and carry a begging bowl?

ST. CLAIRE. (*Coaxing*) You can well afford it.

ROSS. (*Takes money out of his pocket*) I can afford it. I have more than you, although I'm not rich and probably never shall be. (HE *offers the money, then, changing his mind, walks away*) But, if you lend money, as the Indians say, you make a secret enemy.

ST. CLAIRE. (*Angrily*) If you refuse it, you make an open one.

ROSS. (HE *stops and looks at* ST. CLAIRE) Oh, yes?

ST. CLAIRE. (*Sweetly*) Ali.

ROSS. No.

ST. CLAIRE. Please?

ROSS. Stop whimpering!

ST. CLAIRE. (*Roaring*) Bugger you, Ross!

ROSS. (*Cool*) Bugger me? For fifty rupees? Is that value for money?

(THEY *stare at each other*)

ST. CLAIRE. (*Slowly*) You're an odd sort of chap, Ross. I don't know why I do for you.

ROSS. And you, my dear Nelly, have many good points besides your good looks. Your only fault being that you are weak, the least little bit in the world weak. And you carry enough conceit to stock a Viceroy's council.

ST. CLAIRE. (*Threatening*) There are other ways of making money! I am going to sell my commission and settle here.

ROSS. You in India? But you hate the place.

ST. CLAIRE. Well, what am I to do? I can't live in England on a hundred a year, I can't!

ROSS. Well you can't stay here. India has an uncanny way of bringing out extremes in people. We must find you a wife in England. A sweet, pink and white maiden on the government house list, with a great deal of money and some influential connections.

ST. CLAIRE. Alice Napier?

ROSS. That would be a match!

ST. CLAIRE. (*Eagerly*) Will you help me, Ali?

ROSS. (HE *offers his hand*) I will. We must make certain she is clever.

ST. CLAIRE. I don't want her to be clever; why should she be clever?

ROSS. Take my word for it, Neville, the silliest woman can manage a clever man; but it needs a very clever woman to manage a fool.

(HE *turns Upstage and walks toward the gate.* ST. CLAIRE, *sulking, follows him*)

Good evening, Private.

(THEY *have reached the gate. The* PRIVATE *snaps to attention. The* THREE MEN *waiting at the gate are:* PRIVATE JONATHAN SMALL, *a young, clever, working-class soldier.* DURGA DASS, *a small, fawning, low-caste Hindu, and, an Afghan,* WALI DAD, *who is mute.* HE *appears to have only half of his tongue, and his eyes roll incessantly, producing an effect which is not uncomic*)

SMALL. (*A command*) Fall in!

(*The* INDIANS *scramble to their feet and attempt to stand at attention*)

ROSS. Everything in order? Private—

SMALL. Small, sir, Jonathan Small. Good evening, Major. It's my first night on the gates, sir. I feel a bit beef-witted about it all, if you know what I mean.

ROSS. Certainly, Private, let me explain. The fort has a hundred gates, we have just over a hundred white men, so it was decided, by whoever decides these things, that one British soldier and two natives should be posted at each gate. There is a central guardhouse, and if we have serious trouble, Captain St. Claire and I will report to it. We are the night watch for these twenty-five western gates. If you need help, fire your rifle and we will come. If anyone tries to come through the gate, shoot to kill.

ST. CLAIRE. (*Looking coldly at the* TWO INDIANS) Yes. Those black devils are very good at creeping in and murdering sleeping men, women, and children.

SMALL. (*Uncomfortable*) I understand, sir.

ROSS. I will inspect your men, Private.

SMALL. Dress for inspection!

(*The* INDIANS *spread out.* ROSS *goes to* DURGA DASS *and smiles warmly*)

ROSS. Good evening.

DURGA DASS. Greetings, illustrious buckle on the great belt of Queen Victoria!

ROSS. I am Major Alistair Ross and this is Captain Neville St. Claire.

DURGA DASS. (*Salaams to* ST. CLAIRE) Hullo, Inspiration of the Beef-Witted!

SMALL. Fall in, there!

(DURGA DASS *stands at attention*)

Talk sense to the officers. Tell them your name.

DURGA DASS. Ah! I am Durga Dass. (*Pointing to the* SECOND INDIAN) And this is Wali Dad. He is Afghan. Also, he is witless.

WALI DAD. (*Grins and rolls his eyes*) Wa . . . Wa . . .

ST. CLAIRE. (*Looking at* WALI DAD) This man is mad!

DURGA DASS. The witless are under the protection of God. They foretell future events.

SMALL. The man's a mute, sir, but he's all right.

ST. CLAIRE. Fancy!

ROSS. Is he fit for duty?

DURGA DASS. His circumstances are depressed, and he is also down on his luck, poor chap.

ROSS. (*Indicating* DURGA DASS) Now, this fellow makes me homesick. He speaks in English idioms.

DURGA DASS. (*Falls to his knees*) Major, they are the very best of idioms. Top hole, every one.

SMALL. (*To* DURGA DASS) Fall in, there.

(DURGA DASS *rises*)

ST. CLAIRE. (*Restless*) Major, we are behind the schedule.

SMALL. Before you go, sir, could you tell me which gate this is? In case there's any trouble.

ST. CLAIRE. Don't you have a map, man?

SMALL. No, sir. I was marched in column and assigned to the gates. I don't know where I am.

ROSS. As you were!

(*The* MEN *relax*)

You must never speak of Indian things, Small, without looking at a map. (He *takes the regulation map out of his belt and offers it to* SMALL *who reaches for it.* ROSS *drops it on the ground.* SMALL *looks at him for a moment and then picks up the map and studies it*)

ST. CLAIRE. (*Still irritable*) Well, what do we do now?

ROSS. I'm sure these charming gentlemen can entertain us for a few moments.

DURGA DASS. Yes, by Chrickey!

ST. CLAIRE. Oh, Christ! (HE *walks away*)

DURGA DASS. (*To* ROSS) I travel to England once with a thought-reading man from Ceylon. Pull my turban if it is not true! So you see, I am expert at English entertainment.

ROSS. Well, what do you offer?

DURGA DASS. My sister. She is very pink inside like Queen Victoria.

SMALL. (*Quickly*) This is the seventy-fifth gate, sir. I know where I am.

ST. CLAIRE. Well, Allah be praised.

(DURGA DASS *winces*)

Now, Small, I think we should replace this Indian. (*Indicates* WALI DAD) He's not competent.

DURGA DASS. (*Alarmed*) Ah no. Do not take him away. He is powerful. I can prove it.

ST. CLAIRE. How can you prove it?

DURGA DASS. This mutiny. If you know the name of the leader of the rebels, give it to Wali Dad. He will dispatch a Sending and kill him.

SMALL. Major, I must apologize for this nonsense.

ROSS. But I am intrigued, Private. What do you mean by the word "Sending"?

SMALL. It's meant to be a curse . . .

ROSS. (*Cutting him off*) As you were.

DURGA DASS. (*Wide eyed*) A Sending is a horrible arrangement. It is a curse sent by a charmer or wizard, and may take the form of something as insignificant as a piece of paper, or as deadly as a man without a face.

(*A jackal howls. DURGA DASS strikes his breast and mumbles to himself*)

ST. CLAIRE. A man without a face?

SMALL. A leper, sir.

(*There is a gunshot not too far away, followed by the loud barking of two or three dogs*)

ST. CLAIRE. Well, that's real. There are enough of those poor devils in this diseased country.

DURGA DASS. Charmers of the skin-hide caste can dispatch a Sending which, whatever form it takes, will lie on the breast of their enemy by night and kill him.

ST. CLAIRE. (*Beginning to get uncomfortable*) Lie on their breast?

SMALL. It's the symbol of a tombstone, sir.

ST. CLAIRE. It gives me the Willy's.

DURGA DASS. Wali Dad is a charmer. Let him send a Sending for you. Perhaps it will end the mutiny. The God of vengeance will assist.

ST. CLAIRE. (*Crosses to* DURGA DASS—*angrily*) Don't bring God into this. We are Christians and that is our religion. Superstition is religion only to the feeble minded.

DURGA DASS. Certain things are not known to those who eat with forks. It is better to eat with both hands for a while.

ST. CLAIRE. You filthy yellow devil! (ST. CLAIRE *viciously kicks* DURGA DASS *who yells, "Ahi, ahi."* SMALL *is holding* ST. CLAIRE *to keep him from kicking* DURGA DASS *again*)

Private, why are you holding me?

SMALL. I can't have you abusing my men, sir.

ST. CLAIRE. Men? They're a pack of screaming monkeys, from the Maharajah right down to the untouchables, and speaking of that bastard, he forgot to empty the shit bucket today. Why don't you see to that?

SMALL. I will see to it that you don't destroy the good association I have with my men, sir.

ST. CLAIRE. Oh really? Well, I don't associate with fucking niggers.

SMALL. That isn't what the half-castes say. I've heard they bring Indian women to your quarters at all hours.

ST. CLAIRE. Be careful, Small.

SMALL. Oh, I see. The officer does not associate with fucking niggers, except, oddly enough, when he is fucking niggers.

(*The* TWO INDIANS *cower in the gate. With his knee,* ST. CLAIRE *kicks* SMALL *in the groin.* SMALL *bends forward, gasping for breath.* ST. CLAIRE *takes the pistol out of his belt and raises it as if* HE *would smash* SMALL's *head*)

ROSS. St. Claire! What are you doing?

(ST. CLAIRE *immediately releases* SMALL. ROSS *crosses to* ST. CLAIRE *in a cold fury*)

You have been drinking. What else could explain your extraordinary conduct and opinions, which do not reflect, in any way, the feelings of your fellow officers? Now we shall finish our rounds, and then I shall put you on report.

ST. CLAIRE. (HE *salutes*) Yes, Major.

ROSS. (*To* ALL) Gentlemen, I apologize for this officer. (ROSS *turns his back on* ST. CLAIRE *and exits, Left.* ST. CLAIRE *follows him, but first turns back and, glaring at* SMALL, *spits.* SMALL, *deeply disturbed, paces back and forth, still gasping for breath.* WALI DAD *moves Down Center and sits, lotus fashion)*

DURGA DASS. (*To* SMALL) Sahib, will you not rest? Only the devils and the English walk to and fro without reason.

(SMALL *stops pacing and looks at him*)

Be wise. No man can endure watching and great thinking on an empty belly. Sit down, Sahib.

(*Smiling,* WALI DAD *gestures for* SMALL *to sit beside him.* SMALL *does, still holding his rifle.* DURGA DASS *takes a sack of food from his belt*)

Eat, Sahib, eat. Meat is good against sorrow. I also have known. Besides the shadows come and go, they come and go. These be curried eggs—

(SMALL *puts his rifle down, for the first time, in order to take the food. At almost the same moment,* DURGA DASS *darts by him taking the rifle, and* WALI DAD *holds* SMALL's *neck securely in the crook of his arm.* DURGA DASS *points the rifle at* SMALL. WALI DAD *takes a large curved dagger from his belt and presses it against* SMALL's *temple*)

WALI DAD. Sssss. Be still.

SMALL. (*Frozen*) So you can talk.

WALI DAD. So I can. And you can listen, or you can die.

SMALL. Have you joined the rebels? Is this the beginning of an attack? If it is, I will call out and the officers will come.

WALI DAD. They will not come unless the rifle is fired. But do not concern yourself, the fort is safe enough.

SMALL. Then get to the point, man. I don't like having a knife at my head. What do you want? I have no money. I have a Water- bury watch; you can have that.

(WALI DAD *releases* SMALL, *who falls to the ground*)

WALI DAD. (*Standing over him*) I have over a million pounds in jewels. You can have that.

SMALL. Jewels?

WALI DAD. (*Urgently*) Listen to me. Wazir Kahn, the mascot-Maharajah, has joined the rebels, but the English do not know. Now, the Maharajah is a wise man. He would be friends both with the lion and the tiger—with the rebels and with the British Raj. However he trusts no one. He has made such plans that, come what might, he shall keep his fortune. (*Slowly*) All the most precious stones and the choicest pearls that he owns, he has put into a wooden box, and sends it by a trusted servant, who shall bring it, here, this night, to the fort of Agra. This trusted servant now waits not two hundred yards from where you lie, Sahib Small. (HE *gestures to the outside of the gate*) Out there!

SMALL. This is fantasy.

WALI DAD. No, it is kismet. The kismet that happens only once in a hundred years.

SMALL. But how do you know it is true?

WALI DAD. I have a friend who also serves the Maharajah. He explained that I was posted on the gates, and it was thus arranged, for a few rupees, that the servant, Mohammed Singh, should bring the box here, to my gate, and I should let him into the fort.

SMALL. A box . . .

WALI DAD. Full of treasure!

SMALL. Why bring it here?

WALI DAD. To hide it in the Old Quarter.

SMALL. There is no map of the Old Quarter. It's a labyrinth.

WALI DAD. There is one. Mohammed Singh brings, with the treasure, an ancient scroll from the days of the Mogul Empire. With a chosen hiding place, an unfindable place, a place seen only by centipedes and scorpions these many years. We were told to kill you, and instead I offer to make you a partner. In your company we can move freely about the fort, and no one will be curious about the box.

SMALL. (*With dread*) And what happens to the trusted servant?

WALI DAD. Mohammed Singh? If he is taken by the officer Sahibs, he will be hung or shot, and the treasure will be turned over to the English government.

SMALL. I cannot kill for money.

WALI DAD. Durga Dass will cut his throat. There is enough wealth to make us all great chiefs. Think of that.

SMALL. (*Dreaming*) What might I do with a fortune. How my folk will stare when they see their ne'er-do-well coming back from India with pockets full of gold.

WALI DAD. No one can know about the matter, for here we are cut off from all men. What could be better for the purpose? Say then, Sahib, are you with us?

SMALL. I am with you, heart and soul!

(THEY *stand*, WALI DAD *holding* SMALL's *rifle*. THEY *join hands*)

WALI DAD. (*To* DURGA DASS) Go out now, and bring Mohammed Singh to the gate.

(DURGA DASS *runs through the gate. We can hear the patter of his feet against the stone. Dogs begin to bark.*)

(*Hands* SMALL *his rifle*) You see that I trust you, Sahib. Your word, like ours, is not to be broken. We must trust each other for this is a great thing we do. Now, let us prepare.

(THEY *conceal themselves on either side of the gate. The dogs stop barking. Almost in reply, a jackal howls. Then silence. Footsteps can be heard on the stone. A* FIGURE *comes through the gate.* HE *is covered and hooded in dark rags and carries a wooden chest.* HE *comes into the fort while* DURGA DASS *stands behind him in the gate. The* FIGURE *puts down the chest and instantly* DURGA DASS *steps forward, puts his arm over the* MAN's *mouth, and jerking back the head, dagger in hand, expertly cuts the* MAN's *throat. The cloak and hood fall to the ground as the* MAN *reaches for his throat.* HE *has only half a face, and that is wound with strips of cloth: his body is clothed in a white tunic which seems to be made of rags, now soaked with blood.* DURGA DASS *begins to moan. The* MAN *raises his arms; most of the fingers are gone.* HE *is a leper*)

SMALL. Christ in heaven!

WALI DAD. This is not Mohammed Singh.

(DURGA DASS *picks up a lantern and crosses to the* MAN)

It is a leper!

DURGA DASS. A man without a face. A man without a face.

(DURGA DASS *kneels facing the* LEPER. *Directly behind him is the chest of jewels.* HE *stretches out his hands as if to make the image vanish*) Mayah. Mayah. (*Illusion*)

(*The* LEPER *points a hand with one finger at* DURGA DASS *and tries to speak. A terrible rattle comes out of his torn throat and, dying,* HE *falls on* DURGA DASS *who kneeling is driven back until* HE *is forced down and pinned to the chest. The* LEPER *is, in fact, lying on his breast*)

(*Screaming*) The Sending! Ahi!!

(WALI DAD *grabs* SMALL's *rifle and fires into the chest of the* LEPER *whose body arcs into the air and falls, face down, on the ground, freeing* DURGA DASS)

SMALL. The officers will come.

(WALI DAD *holds* DURGA DASS. SMALL *covers the* LEPER's *body with the ragged cloak*)

WALI DAD. (*To* DURGA DASS) Do not think! Pray, meditate.

DURGA DASS. (*Screams at* WALI DAD) Blind ape—blood-worm! Was it for this I left my people and came with you, for the fires of your filthy gold. You said that I should never burn. O Wali Dad, I burn now. I burn. (*Raising his arms*) Have mercy, God of things as they are.

SMALL. (*Kneels by* DURGA DASS) Listen to me. This is no curse! The Maharajah tricked you. He sent a leper with the treasure instead of Mohammed Singh because he knew no one would touch a leper.

DURGA DASS. But I have touched the leper. Behold my face—it

is the face of a cobra. And my arm—it is the arm of an old woman. I am cursed. I have lost my caste. Polluted! Untouchable!

SMALL. (*Urgently*) Control yourself.

DURGA DASS. (*Quietly*) I hear the Genies calling to each other from holes in the sand.

(HE *falls on the ground and rocks back and forth, whimpering and moaning*)

WALI DAD. (*Has been searching the body of the* LEPER) Here is the scroll.

SMALL. Put it away. Now quickly, take the chest outside the gate. I'll drag him as far away as I can. (*Indicating the* LEPER) Don't speak when the officers come.

(WALI DAD *picks up the chest and makes for the gate, as* SMALL *begins to drag the* LEPER *away.* DURGA DASS *moans quietly.* ST. CLAIRE *and* ROSS *enter, pointing their pistols*)

ST. CLAIRE. Who fired that shot? Don't move. Any of you.

ROSS. Private Small, you will explain. (*Pointing to the* LEPER) Who is this man?

SMALL. He tried to come through the gate, sir.

(ST. CLAIRE *goes over to the dead* FIGURE *and looks under the cloak*)

ST. CLAIRE. God almighty. It's a leper.

ROSS. (*Looking at* WALI DAD, *who is frozen in the gate, holding the chest*) What is he holding?

SMALL. (*Thinking furiously*) The Maharajah has joined the rebels, but sent all his jewels to the fort, to hide them here. They are in that chest.

ST. CLAIRE. (*To* ROSS) Can this be true?

SMALL. It is true, sir.

ROSS. I've seen that chest at the palace. (HE *crosses to the*

LEPER *and raises the cloak*) And how did this man come to have his throat cut?

SMALL. (*Pointing to* DURGA DASS) These two were going to kill him and keep the treasure.

ROSS. What went wrong?

SMALL. The Maharajah—crafty bugger. He was to send the treasure with a servant, but he chose a leper instead.

ROSS. And what portion did they offer you, for your assistance?

SMALL. (*Stands at attention*) As you say, sir. (*With a new idea*) Now, if you will accompany me, I will take the chest to the guardhouse, give it to the authorities, and turn myself in.

ROSS. Are you prepared to spend several years on the Andaman Islands? I understand that is going to be a particularly nasty prison.

SMALL. (*Looking at* ROSS *steadily*) I'm prepared for anything.

ST. CLAIRE. (*Who has not taken his eyes off* WALI DAD *and the chest*) There must be a million in that chest.

SMALL. More.

ROSS. (*To* SMALL) Perhaps there is another way to deal with this situation.

SMALL. (*Looking at the* TWO INDIANS) The only way that I will consider, is one that includes all five of us.

ST. CLAIRE. (*Crossing to* DURGA DASS) What's the matter with him? (*To* DURGA DASS) Come on, man, we're not going to hurt you. (HE *tries to pull* DURGA DASS *up by the hand. There is a dagger in the hand, covered with blood*)

SMALL. Jesus, he's killed himself.

ROSS. (*Fascinated*) Because he touched the leper.

SMALL. He said there was a curse, and now he is dead.

ST. CLAIRE. (ST. CLAIRE *looks at* WALI DAD *who still stands in the gate, holding the treasure*) Let me have that.

(WALI DAD *shakes his head no*)

ROSS. Nellie!

SMALL. (*Crosses to* WALI DAD) Give me the scroll.

(ST. CLAIRE *has crossed to* ROSS. THEY *whisper to each other*)

WALI DAD. (*Whispers*) They will kill us, Sahib.

SMALL. No. Give me the scroll.

(WALI DAD *hands him the map* HE *took from the* LEPER. SMALL *tucks it in his uniform*)

I have a way, trust me.

ROSS. We have been making plans.

ST. CLAIRE. Yes, if we are going to be successful, we must act quickly. Small, run to the guardhouse and report that two Indians have ben killed trying to enter the fort.

ROSS. (*To* SMALL) Now hurry, man, lest they come to investigate.

SMALL. (*To* WALI DAD) I will return quickly. (SMALL *dashes Off Right. As soon as* HE *is gone, the* OFFICERS *turn and face* WALI DAD)

WALI DAD. (*Sets the chest down, Center Stage, and sits behind it*) It is no good, is it?

ST. CLAIRE. You can speak!

WALI DAD. I speak too well, and in this new India of white voices it is best to be silent and listen.

ROSS. You were very convincing.

(ST. CLAIRE *walks up to the gate*)

WALI DAD. Do not flatter me, Sahib. I cannot play the clever fool as my friend could.

ST. CLAIRE. What's the matter, man? We are not going to hurt you. (HE *is behind* WALI DAD)

WALI DAD. You mean there is room for me in your plans?

ST. CLAIRE. Of course. (*Slowly* HE *draws his sword*)

WALI DAD. Strange. The bloom of the peace-orchard is upon all the valley, and here is only dust and a great stink.

ROSS. Now, come along, man. We're in this together.

WALI DAD. Together? Are the whites of my eyes clouded? Does the blood beat at my wrist?

ROSS. What of your share?

WALI DAD. The treasure is yours.

(ST. CLAIRE *raises the sword, about to strike*)

ROSS. But why?

WALI DAD. Why? Because white-faced, white-toothed pariahs are not to be trusted with brown skin. (HE *turns, screaming, draws his dagger, and makes to cut* ST. CLAIRE's *face.* ST. CLAIRE *backs off.* WALI DAD *darts through the gate*)

ROSS. (*To* ST. CLAIRE) Kill him!

(ST. CLAIRE *takes out his pistol. We can hear the patter of* WALI DAD's *feet.* ST. CLAIRE *kneels in the gate and fires. The footsteps stop. Dogs bark*)

ST. CLAIRE. Done! (*To* ROSS) What about Small?

ROSS. I must have time to think.

ST. CLAIRE. (*Quietly*) Why share three ways?

ROSS. We *are* greedy!

ST. CLAIRE. He's an Indian lover.

ROSS. We will never succeed if he is with us. We must get rid of him.

(*A jackal howls nearby*)

ST. CLAIRE. Christ! Ali. Three deaths. What I mean is . . . Well, this curse business. Do you think there's anything in it?

ROSS. I heard of a family, once, who had a curse on its first-born.

ST. CLAIRE. What happened?

ROSS. It turned out to be the plumbing. As soon as new drains were put into the house the curse was lifted, I believe. I never knew the family myself.

(*The* TWO MEN *laugh, then, slowly, their eyes are drawn to the chest*)

Shall I open it? Will you look on your future, Nelly?

ST. CLAIRE. I'm afraid.

ROSS. Of what?

ST. CLAIRE. It will be empty.

ROSS. (*Crossing to it*) Some people say there is no romance in India. These people are wrong. Our lives hold quite as much romance as is good for us and sometimes more. (*With his sword point,* HE *deftly breaks the lock and opens the lid.* THEY *gasp. We cannot see the jewels, not yet, but we can see their reflection: a glow of colored flecks which plays on the faces of the* MEN)

ST. CLAIRE. (*Transported*) All the stars of heaven in a box.

(SMALL *runs in from the Right.* THEY *do not hear him*)

And it's ours, Ali. Yours and mine! (ST. CLAIRE *picks up a large, glittering stone*)

ROSS. Put it down!

(ST. CLAIRE *does.* ROSS *sees* SMALL. ST. CLAIRE *slams the lid of the chest. There is an awkward moment*)

SMALL. (*Breathlessly*) It's all done. They will send some men to collect the bodies. We must hurry. (HE *looks around*) Where's Wali Dad?

ST. CLAIRE. He ran away.

SMALL. I thought I heard a shot.

ROSS. There was a shot. We couldn't let him carry this tale to his friends.

SMALL. (*Desperate*) Oh, God forgive me. I promised to look after him. I shouldn't have left him with you.

ST. CLAIRE. You can't trust them.

SMALL. *(Terrified)* And you? Can I trust you?

(The THREE MEN *look at each other. Suddenly,* SMALL *grows calm)*

Yes. I think I can. Without me, you can't keep that chest.

ROSS. What do you mean?

SMALL. If you kill me, where do you think you're going to hide it?

ROSS. Go on.

SMALL. *(Desperate)* The old Maharajah knew a thing or two. This is his home. He studied this fort. Wouldn't you say that we should follow his plan?

ROSS. Which was?

SMALL. He sent a scroll, a map of the old quarter. On it is marked the one place in this whole rabbit-warren where the treasure will be absolutely safe. And I know where it is.

ST. CLAIRE. Show the scroll to us.

SMALL. Don't be a fool. I put it in a safe place on the way to the guardhouse. Now you need me as much as I need you.

ST. CLAIRE. I think not. We can hide the chest in our rooms.

SMALL. Are you in your rooms all day? Can you trust your Indian servants?

ROSS. He's right, Nelly. They'd find it in a minute.

ST. CLAIRE. He's not right. He can't be! There must be another way.

SMALL. You had better decide quickly! The half-castes will be coming to collect the bodies.

ROSS. What do you propose?

SMALL. I shall hide the chest for you now, according to the scroll. When we return to England, you can transport it with your baggage, and we can divide it equally over there. They never search the officers' trunks, but they'd search mine.

ROSS. True.

SMALL. So we need each other. Do you agree? (*Pause*) Well?

(ROSS *nods, looks at* ST. CLAIRE. HE *nods*)
Good! Now I propose a Covenant.

ST. CLAIRE. What for?

SMALL. A gesture of good faith.

ROSS. You mean a paper? A paper saying "We the undersigned
have committed two murders, and caused a suicide while amass-
ing a great fortune, but in future, we will try in every way we
can, to be kind to each other" . . . You want us to put our
names on something like that?

SMALL. I don't want your names. I want your blood.

ST. CLAIRE. What do you mean?

SMALL. I mean a blood oath, Captain. An oath sworn in your
own blood, which you break at your peril.

ST. CLAIRE. That's sacreligious! You're as mad as the Indians.

SMALL. Will you do it? Yes or No?

(ROSS *crosses to* DURGA DASS *and takes the dagger from
the dead man's hand*)

ST. CLAIRE. Ali, don't do it!

ROSS. Be quiet. It's the only way. (HE *wipes it first, then plunges
it into his wrist, drawing blood. Music plays*)

SMALL. (To St. Claire) Thank you, Major Ross. Now you, Captain St. Claire.

ST. CLAIRE. (*Afraid*) It's perverse . . . It makes me sick . . .
It's evil.

ROSS. You will find, if you want to make any money in this
world, it is not always wise to be disturbed by what we call evil.
And you want money, Nelly. That's all you ever want. Do it!

(HE *hands him the dagger*)

ST. CLAIRE. I can't. I can't. I'm getting the shakes . . .

SMALL. Here. Take this. (*From his pocket* HE *offers a pill*)

ST. CLAIRE. What is it?

SMALL. Clean Alwa opium. It will steady your nerves . . . Now do it. Captain St. Claire!

(ST. CLAIRE *takes the opium and, falteringly, cuts his wrist. The blood flows.* SMALL *seizes the dagger and begins to cut his. Lights fade*)

ROSS. Now . . . What shall we swear?

(*The stage is black*)

SCENE TWO

221-B Baker Street. 1887—30 years later.

The music changes to a solitary violin. The stage is dark and covered with fog. Through the fog, at the back of the stage, a MAN plays the violin we hear. Tall and thin, with a hawklike face, HE wears a long silk dressing gown, and walks toward us. This is SHERLOCK HOLMES, the world's foremost consulting detective.

The fog lifts and we see the interior of Baker Street. Two windows Stage Right with a vista of gray London fog. Stage Left a fireplace to which a pile of correspondence is attached with a long dagger. A chaise longue by the fireplace and further into the room a basket chair. HOLMES stands alone in the room. Suddenly HE flings the instrument into the basket chair, and crosses to the breakfast table, Stage Right. From a box on the table, HE takes a syringe and a phial of liquid. HE fills the syringe, and rolling back the sleeve of his dressing gown HE is about to inject his arm when a MAN rushes into the room through the doorway almost Center Stage. The MAN carries a pistol which HE seems to be pointing directly at HOLMES. The TWO MEN stare at each other, one holding a hypodermic, the OTHER a pistol.

BOTH MEN *are in their early thirties.*

HOLMES. (*Looking at the pistol*) Are you going to kill me?

MAN. (*Looking at the syringe*) You seem quite capable of accomplishing that without my assistance.

HOLMES. You are developing a certain vein of pawky humor, Watson, against which I must learn to guard myself.

WATSON. (*Looking at the pistol*) Ah! Excuse me! I was officiating at a foot race for medical students in Pimlico. (HE *puts the pistol on the mantel.* WATSON *takes some letters from his pocket*) The post is here.

HOLMES. You know where to put it.

(WATSON *removes the dagger from the mantel, adds the letters HE carries to the pile, and impales them with the dagger*)

WATSON. Holmes, I must speak with you.

(*Homes looks at him*)

I don't know whether it is the claret which I have taken with my lunch, or the exasperation produced by the extreme deliberation of your manner, but I suddenly feel I can hold out no longer.

HOLMES. (*Holding up the needle*) I see. You wish to try it.

WATSON. (*Indignant*) Try it indeed! I cannot afford to put that kind of strain upon *my* constitution.

HOLMES. I suppose you are right. I find it, however, so clarifying to the mind, that its secondary, destructive action is a matter of small moment.

WATSON. Is it? But consider. Count the cost. It is a pathological and morbid process, which involves tissue-change, and may, at last leave a permanent weakness. Surely the game is hardly worth the candle.

HOLMES. (*Pacing*) My mind rebels at stagnation. Give me problems, give me work, give me the most abstruse cryptogram or the most intricate analysis, and I am in my own proper atmosphere. But I abhor the dull routine of existence. I am *frustrated,* Watson.

WATSON. (*Indicating the syringe*) That is not the solution.

HOLMES. Nonsense. Frustrate a Frenchman, he will die of combustion; a Dane, he will shoot himself; an American, he will shoot you, establish a million dollar trust for your relatives. Then he will die of an ulcer. A seven-per-cent solution of Cocaine is *my* solution.

WATSON. And it is my contention that far from clarifying the brain, these stimulants cloud it, and cause it to function at a small percentage of its full reasoning power.

HOLMES. (*About to inject himself*) Rubbish!

WATSON. Would you think me impertinent if I were to put my theory to a test?

HOLMES. On the contrary. I should be delighted to look into any mental problem which you might submit to me. (*Holding up the syringe*) And in the first delicious onslaught of this extraordinary property. (HE *rolls back his left shirt cuff and injects his wrist.* WATSON *looks away with distaste, as* HOLMES *falls back on the chaise with a long sigh of satisfaction*)

WATSON. I have heard you say that it is difficult for a man to have any object with him in daily use, without leaving the impress of his individuality upon it. Now, I have here a watch which has recently come into my possession. Would you let me have an opinion as to the character or habits of the late owner?

(HOLMES *takes the watch, looks hard at the dial, opens the back, takes a magnifying glass from his pocket and* peers *through it, then snaps the watch shut and hands it back. Through the following dialogue,* HE *fights hard to maintain continuity of speech and idea, momentarily lapsing into short cocaine-trances*)

HOLMES. There are hardly any data. The watch has been recently cleaned, which robs me of my most suggestive facts.

WATSON. (*Smugly*) You are right. It was cleaned before being sent to me. I must point out, however, that you have put forward a most lame and impotent excuse to cover your failure.

HOLMES. Though unsatisfactory, my research has not been entirely without success. It is a fifty Guinea watch, hence, it was owned by a gentleman. He was, alas, possessed of untidy habits. He was left with good prospects, but he threw away his chances, lived for some time in poverty with occasional short intervals of prosperity, and finally taking to drink, he died. The watch has, in fact, been in the hands of your elder brother.

WATSON. (*Angrily*) This is unworthy of you, Holmes. You have made inquiries into the history of my unhappy brother, and you now pretend to deduce this knowledge in some fanciful way. You cannot expect me to believe that you have read all this from his old watch.

HOLMES. (*With sincerity*) My dear friend, pray accept my apologies. Viewing the matter as an abstract problem, I had forgotten how personal and painful a thing it might be to you. I assure you, however, that I never even knew that you had a brother until you handed me the watch.

WATSON. Then how in the name of all that is wonderful did you get these facts? They are absolutely correct in every particular. This is not guesswork.

HOLMES. No, I never guess. It is a shocking habit, destructive to the logical faculty. I began by stating that your brother was careless. When you observe the lower part of that watchcase, you notice it is cut and marked all over from the habit of keeping the other hard objects, such as coins and keys, in the same pocket. It is customary for pawnbrokers in England, when they take a watch, to scratch the number of the ticket with a pin point upon the inside of the case. There are no fewer than four such numbers visible to my lens. Inference—that your brother was often at low water, but, he had occasional bursts of prosperity, or he could not have redeemed the pledge. Look at the inner plate, which contains the keyhole.

(WATSON *does*)

There are thousands of scratches all round the hole, marks where the key has slipped. You will never see a drunkard's watch without them. He winds it at night, and leaves these traces of his unsteady hand. Lastly, you said the watch had come into your possession, meaning you did not buy it. The initials H.W. on the back suggest your own name. If the watch was left to you as a legacy, and since your father has been dead these many years, it can only mean it is a bequest from your late brother. Where is the mystery in all this? (HE *falls exhausted onto the chaise*)

WATSON. I apologize, Holmes. In future, I will have more faith in your marvelous faculty.

HOLMES. I am the slave of my faculty. I cannot live without brainwork. What else is there to live for?

(*There is an urgent knocking at the door.* WATSON *opens it. A* YOUNG WOMAN *of great beauty rushes into the room. This is* IRENE ST. CLAIRE, *daughter of* NEVILLE ST. CLAIRE. *Unlike her* FATHER, SHE *is mild-mannered, charming and possessed of an appealing and unshakable directness. At the moment* SHE *is deeply distressed*)

IRENE. I am Irene St. Claire.

HOLMES. And I am Sherlock Holmes. (*Indicating* WATSON) And this—is Doctor Watson, my friend and—

(IRENE *staggers and almost falls.* WATSON *rushes to her*)

WATSON. Holmes!

IRENE. (*Trying to regain her composure*) Please forgive me, Gentlemen! I have been frightened, almost out of my wits!

HOLMES. Pray, Miss St. Claire, take a moment or two to compose yourself.

IRENE. (*To* WATSON) The streets are so crowded because of Her Majesty's Jubilee. It took hours to get here. (*To* HOLMES) I have read of your exploits, Mr. Holmes, but I feared you would not wish to be of service to me.

HOLMES. Because you have no money!

IRENE. How can you possibly know that?

HOLMES. In the indications of female poverty, there can be no disguise. No woman dresses below herself from caprice.

WATSON. (*Angrily to* HOLMES) You really are an automaton —a calculating machine—there is something positively inhuman in you at times. How can you be so rude?

HOLMES. It is of the first importance not to allow your judgment to be biased by personal qualities.

IRENE. Dr. Watson, you are very kind, but I prefer absolute candor. To love the truth is to refuse to let oneself be saddened by it.

HOLMES. (*Looking at her with interest*) Miss St. Claire, I beg that you will lay before us everything that may help us in forming an opinion upon this matter. As to reward, my profession is its own reward, and my expenses are somewhat defrayed for the moment. My last client was a sort of king.

WATSON. Shall I order you a cup of hot coffee, for I observe that you are shivering?

IRENE. It is not cold which makes me shiver.

WATSON. What, then?

IRENE. It is fear, Dr. Watson. It is terror!

HOLMES. I am all attention.

IRENE. (SHE *reaches into her handbag and takes out a piece of paper*) This arrived in the post, yesterday morning. (SHE *holds it up. This is the center piece of what will later be called the crucifer. It is the center section of the regulation map from Scene 1. At the top and bottom an arc is drawn, in the center a cross in what appears to be brown paint*)

HOLMES. (*Taking it*) Dated June 1857. Exactly thirty years ago. Curious.

IRENE. The thing is innocent enough. It might be the work of a child. But when my father opened it, he fell unconscious to the floor, badly cutting his head. I put him in his bed, where he remained for the rest of the day. He would not talk about it. That evening, I heard him scream. (SHE *shivers*) I ran to his room, and it was there that I had the shock of my life. He was cowering in the corner like a frightened child, muttering over and over again, something about a curse. It was pitiful. And then I saw it.

HOLMES. Please, go on. What did you see?

IRENE. Hanging on the outside of the window. A hideous shadow, like a large cross stretched over the pane. It was too small to be a man, and yet, I am sure that it was substantial. Then it vanished.

HOLMES. What did you do?

IRENE. I sent for the police. They came, searched the house and the yard. The window is on the second floor. Their conclusion, naturally enough, was that we had been the victims of an hallucination.

WATSON. (*Knowingly*) Typical.

IRENE. Mr. Holmes, I am not an hysteric, and I am not superstitious. I am certain that I saw it.

HOLMES. I believe you absolutely, Miss St. Claire.

IRENE. Thank heaven! The police were kind enough to leave a

man to watch the house. This morning, when I looked in his room, my father was gone.

HOLMES. (*Holding the crucifer*) And you have no idea as to the significance of this paper?

IRENE. None. Oh, it breaks my heart to think of him, alone and terrified, wandering in the fog.

HOLMES. Do you have any idea where he might have gone?

IRENE. I—(SHE *is embarrassed*) Yes, I do. Dr. Watson, Mr. Holmes, I hope you will not turn me away.

HOLMES. My dear young woman, why should we do that?

IRENE. My father is an opium addict.

WATSON. (*Looking at* HOLMES) I am sorry to hear it.

IRENE. That is how the little money we have has been spent.

WATSON. (*Still looking at* HOLMES) It sounds to me as if your father should be soundly thrashed.

IRENE. (*Sharply*) Dr. Watson, I love my father. I tell you his story because you must know the truth if you are to advise me. But if you malign him—I cannot bear it. I will be forced to seek help elsewhere.

HOLMES. I understand, Miss St. Claire. *Your* loyalty is admirable.

IRENE. It is not blind loyalty. Something happened to him, long ago, that permanently affected his heart and mind. It is a singular sort of depression which comes over him.

HOLMES. And it was these moods that drove him to opium?

IRENE. That drove him to addiction. As you surely know, there are places in the east end of London, where one may go to breathe in the poison.

HOLMES. Indeed, Miss St. Claire. Limehouse. But these places are not free of charge. How can a man without money support such a habit?

IRENE There is a Major Alistair Ross who lives at Maidenhead in a gloomy house called Pondicherry Lodge. Whenever we find ourselves reduced to our last farthing, my father goes to him and returns with five or ten pounds, and when this money runs out, he repeats the process.

HOLMES. (*Has been studying the crucifer*) Miss St. Claire, would you excuse me for a few moments? I would like to examine this paper in my room. I keep one or two chemicals that might throw some light on its origins.

IRENE. I would be grateful if you did.

(HOLMES *goes through the door Left to the bedrooms.* WATSON, *uneasily left with* IRENE, *sits and smiles*)

WATSON. I hope your mind is more at ease, Miss St. Claire.

IRENE. (*With charm*) Dr. Watson, I have done nothing but snap at you like a turtle since we met.

WATSON. If I may take the liberty of contradicting you, it is quite the contrary, you have opened my eyes.

IRENE. How?

WATSON. I was beginning to believe that all the young women of London were lisping, coy simpletons, with barely enough sense to take care of the yapping little dogs they seem to take with them wherever they go. Your honesty and courage, in the face of hardships that would drive an ordinary young woman mad, fill me with awe. You are extraordinary!

IRENE. (*Angrily*) I do not wish to be extraordinary. I wish I were a simpleton, without a care in the world. (SHE *bursts into tears*) Forgive me! What can you think of me? It just occurred to me that I have no friends. Since our circumstances forced us to move to Camberwell, I never see anyone of my own age or position. Our neighbors think us too grand, and will not associate with us; while our friends, now think us too low, and have dropped us. It is a comedy. And I find myself, seeking help from two perfect strangers. Until this moment, I, at least, had my pride.

(HE *takes her hand.* SHE *looks for a moment as if* SHE *will take it away, but* SHE *does not*)

WATSON. And you have it still. The seat of pride is in the heart, and only there.

IRENE. (*Looking at him*) Do not pity me.

WATSON. But I do, and I shall. We pity in others, only those evils which we have ourselves experienced. I have just lost a brother. The story of your father was like his own.

IRENE. What is your name?

WATSON. John. Will you call me John? And will you think of *me* as your friend?

IRENE. (*Meeting his eyes*)Your eyes are kind.

WATSON. Is that so rare?

IRENE. I have seen eyes that threaten like loaded pistols.

(THEY *look at each other*—HOLMES *bursts into the room holding the piece of the crucifer*)

HOLMES. Miss St. Claire, did your father serve in India?

IRENE. Yes, Mr. Holmes. How did you guess that?

HOLMES. You mentioned another military man, a Major Ross. And this paper is Indian papyrus, not available in England. My dear, I do not wish to alarm you, but I think we should leave for Camberwell at once. Perhaps your father has returned, and, if not, we may find a clue to his whereabouts.

IRENE. I did not mention that we live in Camberwell, Mr. Holmes. (SHE *looks at* WATSON) Not to you.

HOLMES. They are digging up the area around the Post Office in Camberwell, are they not? The red clay on the soles of your boots is indigenous only to that area of London.

IRENE. Mr. Holmes, you take my breath away.

WATSON. It is amazing!

HOLMES. It is elementary. (*Holding up crucifer*) But this is not.

WATSON. What have you discovered, Holmes?

HOLMES. I cannot say.

(*There is a roll of thunder—a storm is gathering*)

It is dangerous to reason from insufficient data. Fetch an umbrella, Watson.

(WATSON *goes through the door Center*)

There's a storm brewing. Miss St. Claire, I can understand your terror.

IRENE. What do you mean?

HOLMES. There is a mystery about this which stimulates the imagination. Where there is no imagination there is no horror. The markings on this paper were made with blood.

WATSON. (*Returning with two umbrellas*) Holmes, perhaps you could manage to be less outspoken. Are you all right, Miss St. Claire?

IRENE. My family seems to be in the grasp of some inexorable evil, which no foresight and no precaution can guard against. I would almost believe that we are all cursed.

HOLMES. Watson, be kind enough to fetch a cab from the stand, a fourwheeler.

(WATSON *exits through the door, Center*)

Miss St. Claire, I want you to tell me exactly what you mean by that.

(THEY *move Down to the edge of the stage. Music plays. Baker Street fades behind them, and the fog moves in*)

(*To* IRENE) Why did you use the word cursed?

IRENE. It began thirty years ago, when my father returned from India. He had no money. He married my mother, Alice Napier, who had a considerable fortune—not less than ten thousand pounds a year. People said this was the reason for the marriage, but I know that he loved her. Almost from the beginning, he gambled heavily, and chased after adventurous business investments. In a few short years our fortune was gone. Another year or two saw the seizure of our estate by creditors. As a child, I remember being fussed over and dressed by servants, and then, almost overnight, moved to a small, dingy house in Camberwell, where my mother and I had to do all the work. Last year my mother was taken from us. She died in a railway accident near Crewe. Do you believe in the supernatural, Mr. Holmes?

HOLMES. I do not discount it.

WATSON. (*Entering Left*) I have a cab.

IRENE. I will not try to thank you.

(*As* THEY *go*)

HOLMES. But I will thank you, Miss St. Claire, and our lucky fate which has rescued me from the insufferable fatigues of idleness.

(THEY *are gone. The stage is dark*)

SCENE THREE

Part One

Pondicherry Lodge, in Maidenhead.

A great shaft of white light pours through a large, mullioned window of arched, Indian design, which is in the Center of the stage. The light illuminates a sitting room reflecting a taste for Indian objects and decor. Pollard lime trees with spiky branches stand outside the window.

On Stage Left stands an elaborate screen of Indian design, and on the Right, a similarly designed fireplace. Near the window there is a table which contains two candlesticks and a newspaper. The only furniture in the room is a high-backed chair; there is nothing which suggests wealth. A wheel chair stands empty in the Center of the stage.

It is evening of the same day. The storm has moved to Maidenhead and thunder rolls periodically in long peals.

A young man in livery, pokes his head through the door, Stage Left. This is BIRDY JOHNSON.

BIRDY JOHNSON *enters.* HE *is a young Cockney of surly disposition and limited resources, who is manservant to* MAJOR ALISTAIR ROSS. HE *looks at the empty room and calls out.*

JOHNSON. Major. Major, sir? (*Stealthily,* He *crosses to the wheel chair and begins to examine it. A man steps out from behind the screen. It is* ROSS, *now in his fifties, but looking a great deal older.* HE *can barely walk without a cane, his health appears to be ruined, and his cool manner from the first scene has been replaced with an irritable, waspish sarcasm. His fingers are covered with jewels*)

ROSS. (*Approaching* JOHNSON *with the aid of his cane*) Caught!

JOHNSON. (*Frightened*) Sir?

ROSS. What are you about, you dog?

JOHNSON. Just tidying up, sir.

ROSS. You are a fox, Birdy, you are an exceedingly cunning fox, with that demure visage of yours.

JOHNSON. I will not be called a fox, sir.

ROSS. (*Imitating him*) "I will not be called a fox, sir." Really, Birdy, your wit is of the shallowest order. It does not reach even to a saw or a proverb. A sucking babe might challenge you. Well? What are you staring at, boy?

JOHNSON. I wasn't staring.

ROSS. (*Strikes him with his cane*) There's a lesson for you!

JOHNSON. I won't endure it. I won't be knocked about in this way, I won't!

ROSS. (*Sitting in his wheel chair*) And what will you do, run to your mother?

JOHNSON. (*At the mention of his mother* HE *shrinks*) I'm sorry, sir.

ROSS. That's better, dear boy. Your mother will be spared for today. Now why did you come in here?

JOHNSON. There's a peddler at the door, sir.

ROSS. A peddler? Give him a shilling out of your own pocket if he moves you. That is what these fellows come for.

JOHNSON. He said he had something of value to sell. Something with jewels. You told me never to turn away anyone—

ROSS. (*Sharply*) Your voice is like a pistol crack today. Pray, spare me the sound of it by not repeating things to me which I have already said to you. Where is the peddler?

JOHNSON. (*Indicating the door*) Just outside, sir.

ROSS. Well, bring him in. (ROSS *takes snuff.*

JOHNSON *opens the door and shows the* PEDDLER *into the room*)

JOHNSON. This way. (HE *leaves.*

The PEDDLER *is old, dressed in cloak and hat. An eye patch covers one eye, and his right leg has been replaced by a wooden stump. It sounds on the floor boards as* HE *walks*)

PEDDLER. Good day to you, Master.

ROSS. You are a stranger about these parts?

PEDDLER. Aye, just put ashore, at Gravesend.

ROSS. And what's your business in this part of the country?

PEDDLER. I hope to sell one or two things acquired in my travels.

ROSS. You've been to sea?

PEDDLER. Aye, Master, and I have only now lately come up the river from an Indian voyage.

ROSS. India?

PEDDLER. Aye, Master, that great four-square sink of humanity.

ROSS. And you have something to show me, I understand? Something with jewels.

PEDDLER. Nothing that can match the opulence of the dressings on your fingers.

ROSS. (*Looking at his own fingers appreciatively*) We'll see! What have you to sell?

PEDDLER. (*Tapping something in his pocket*) A small casket.

ROSS. I will examine it in the window, while the light lasts. Come with me. (ROSS *wheels himself to the window. The* PEDDLER *follows him and hands him the box. It is shaped like a coffin*)

(*Looking at the box*) What's this stuff?

PEDDLER. Pearls and hand-hammered brass. (HE *leaves the window and begins to examine the room*)

ROSS. It's dull workmanship. No good at all.

PEDDLER. Look at the content—not the box. Open it.

ROSS. (*Takes out a dagger*) A Kris!

PEDDLER. Yes. Capable of inflicting the most ferocious wounds. It's marvelous workmanship, don't you agree? And very rare . . . Do you have a safe to put it in?

ROSS. What's that to you?

PEDDLER. Nothing at all. But with real rubies and diamonds you can't be too careful. (HE *is by the fireplace*)

ROSS. What are you doing there?

PEDDLER. Looking about, sir, just looking about. Taking stock of a gentleman's sitting room. Not much to see, is there, in the way of display? Not if you had to sit in here all day and just look about you. How did you lose the use of your legs, if I may be so bold as to ask?

ROSS. Damn your impertinence! How did you lose yours, come to that?

PEDDLER. It was chewed off.

ROSS. By what?

PEDDLER. The mouth of greed.

ROSS. What do you mean?

PEDDLER. Greed, sir, is greed. You know what greed is, surely?

ROSS. I think you're mad.

PEDDLER. (*Crosses to him and takes the Kris*) Perhaps I am. Perhaps I came here not to sell but to buy.

ROSS. What?

PEDDLER. Your life. (HE *raises the Kris to* ROSS's *face*) Perhaps I am a virtuoso in the art of murder and am desirous of improving myself in its details. Perhaps I am enamored of your vast surface of throat, to which I am determined to be a customer.

(JOHNSON *comes in. The* PEDDLER *backs away from* ROSS *who is trembling*)

JOHNSON. Captain St. Claire is here, sir. I put him in the library.

ROSS. (*Relieved*) Clever boy! You're a very clever boy! (*Indicating the* PEDDLER) Show this man out. And if you see him again, take a club to him. (*To the* PEDDLER) Try to intimidate me, will you? Get out! Get out!

(*The* PEDDLER *walks to the door, his stump sounding on the floor boards.* ROSS *bangs his own legs against the chair,*

*imitating the sound of the wooden leg. At the door, the PED-
DLER turns and looks at him*)

PEDDLER. (*Laughing heartily,* HE *slaps his wooden leg*) Good
day to you, Master. (HE *leaves*)

ROSS. (*To* JOHNSON) Bring Nelly to me. Hurry, boy, hurry!

(JOHNSON *leaves.* ROSS, *agitated, wheels his chair to the
window and watches. The* PEDDLER *passes the window on
the outside, by the Pollard lime trees.* HE *waves merrily at*
ROSS, *who, confused, spins his chair away from the window.*
ST. CLAIRE *enters the room. Like* ROSS, HE *looks older
than his fifty-odd years. Dissipation and anxiety are clearly
visible in his face, but* HE *still retains a great deal of his for-
mer vigor. At the moment,* HE *is frightened*)

JOHNSON. (*At the door*) Captain St. Claire, sir. (HE *leaves*)

ST. CLAIRE. Can that servant of yours be trusted?

ROSS. What kind of a greeting is that, Nelly? I haven't seen you
for months.

ST. CLAIRE. Can he be trusted?

ROSS. Of course.

(JOHNSON *enters with a tray of whiskey and glasses which*
HE *places on the table, Stage Right*)

You remember his mother, she was once housekeeper here, the
sour-faced bitch.

(*Stunned,* JOHNSON *turns and faces him*)

I put temptation in her way, in the form of money, and, of
course, she took it. You see, I had my eye on her handsome little son. Then I demanded she sign a confession, which is now in
my solicitor's files. If anything happens to me, or if Birdy mis-
behaves, that confession goes to the police and Birdy's mother
goes to prison. Does that answer your question?

(ST. CLAIRE *crosses to the table and pours himself a large
whiskey.* JOHNSON *crosses to* ROSS *and spinning the wheel
chair, snarls in* ROSS's *face*)

(*In mock surprise*) Birdy!

JOHNSON. You promised. You said you'd never tell anyone. It was between us. You and me!

ROSS. (*Amusing himself*) I have a wild thing in the house.

JOHNSON. (*Through clenched teeth*) Perhaps you do, sir. Instead of a fox, it may be a tiger you have in your house, sir.

ROSS. (*Looks him over carefully, his eyes resting on* BIRDY's *gloved hands*) A cat in gloves, Birdy, catches no mice.

(JOHNSON *looks at him with loathing, and leaves the room.* ROSS *turns to* ST. CLAIRE *who stands by the table pale and shaking*)

What's the matter with you, Nelly? You look terrible.

ST. CLAIRE. The curse. I've seen it. A monstrous cross at my window!

ROSS. It is the opium, my dear. It has bewildered you and obscured your perception.

ST. CLAIRE. No. There's something else. Small is alive.

ROSS. What?

ST. CLAIRE. His piece of the oath. It arrived in the post yesterday. It was sent from London.

ROSS. (*Placating*) If he is alive, which I doubt, he doesn't want us. He is compelled by the same thing that has governed our lives for the past thirty years. It has driven you to ruin, and it has obsessed my every waking moment.

ST. CLAIRE. (*Shouting*) Give it to him, for Christ's sake. He's earned it! If he comes here, take him to the bank where you keep it and give it to him.

ROSS. (*Not moving*) I will never give it up. And it is not in a bank.

ST. CLAIRE. (*Terrified*) I knew it! It is here, isn't it? In this house!

ROSS. (*Moving*) In this room!

(ST. CLAIRE *flings himself in front of the wheel chair*)

ST. CLAIRE. But I gave up my share. I told you I didn't want anything to do with it. I gave it to you. I freed myself from the curse.

ROSS. Yes, you freed yourself. You took the burden of guilt from your own conscience. You gave up the treasure. But you came begging to it, didn't you, whenever you wanted money. All these years, after you threw away the Napier fortune, which I helped you to win, you have always come back to it, haven't you? And I have kept it. I have watched over it and kept it pure.

ST. CLAIRE. (*Loud*) But you do not spend it. Why must you keep it? You do not enjoy it.

ROSS. (*Louder*) It's the having! The possession alone is my strength, the energy of my soul—the warmth of my blood. Not to have my wasted lifetime back again would I give up the great Agra Treasure. (*Slowly, grotesquely,* HE *sinks to his knees and opens the front of the wheel chair, under the seat*) Why do you think my legs failed me? I no longer needed them. I am content to *sit* in this empty room, guarding it, like a dragon in a cave. Here, night and day, I have gazed upon it; my soul has drunk its radiance. (HE *pulls the chest out of the wheel chair onto the floor*)

ST. CLAIRE. (*Jumping up*) I don't want to see.

ROSS. You are not worthy to see, even from far off, the luster of the most precious gems that were ever concocted in the laboratory of nature.

ST. CLAIRE. Ali, I beg you! Put it back.

ROSS. (*With his arms around the chest*) Are you frightened? I can remember your last glance at it, just as the iron-plated lid fell down. And ever since, through thirty years, it has been blazing in secret, and gathering its splendor against the glorious moment, when you look upon it again. Let it be now! It will flash upon you like the noonday sun.

ST. CLAIRE. (*Crying out*) I won't look!!

ROSS. Then shade your eyes.

(ST. CLAIRE *covers his face, sobbing.* ROSS *opens the chest; a glow fills the room, but we cannot see the jewels*)

When I die, it will be buried with me forever. Will it not make a rare lamp for a sepulcher? Will it not burn brightly in a tomb? There shall it flame for ages, keeping bright my memory. The memory of a hero.

ST. CLAIRE. You are insane.

(JOHNSON *stands in the doorway*)

ROSS. (*Slams the lid of the chest down*) Get out!

JOHNSON. There's Mr. Sherlock Holmes at the door.

ROSS. (*Putting the chest back in the chair*) Sherlock Holmes? Who is that?

ST. CLAIRE. A detective.

ROSS. That crank who attracts attention in the newspapers?

BIRDY. There's a doctor with him, and the Captain's daughter.

ST. CLAIRE. Irene.

ROSS. Well bring them here. (*Looks at* ST. CLAIRE) Is this your doing?

ST. CLAIRE. No, but I'm glad he's here.

ROSS. (*Sitting in the wheel chair*) Let me do the talking. I will get rid of them.

ST. CLAIRE. (*Covering* ROSS *with the lap rug*) Let them stay. Let them help us. Small may be out there!

ROSS. If he is, I am glad. It will be settled one way or another.

(HOLMES, WATSON *and* IRENE *enter the room led by* JOHNSON. IRENE *runs to* ST. CLAIRE)

IRENE. Oh, my dear, let me look at you.

ST. CLAIRE. Irene, did you bring these people here?

IRENE. Yes. They are my friends. They will help us.

HOLMES. (*To* ROSS) Major Ross, I assume? I am Sherlock Holmes—

ROSS. (*Cutting him off*) Sherlock Holmes. The murder fancier? Whatever can have brought you to Maidenhead? Why aren't you in London, Mr. Holmes, that great cesspool of crime?

WATSON. (*Shocked*) My word!

HOLMES. It is my belief, Major Ross, founded upon my experience, that the vilest alleys of London do not present a more dreadful record of sin than does the smiling and beautiful countryside.

(ROSS *backs away from him and turns to* IRENE.

ST. CLAIRE *goes to the table and pours himself a huge whiskey*)

ROSS. Nelly, is this your daughter?

IRENE. Yes, Major Ross. We have met before.

ROSS. But you've grown so beautiful. Ah, you are your father's daughter. Almost as beautiful as he once was.

WATSON. (*Stunned*) I'll be bound.

ROSS. And now his grace has faded.

WATSON. See here, Major Ross!

IRENE. (*With a smile*) Yes. But when my father's grace faded in my eyes, I found it again in my heart.

ROSS. Charming! Charming! But what an honor. (*Wheeling himself around the room in high spirits*) There hasn't been a woman in this house since dear Birdy's mother left my employ.

(HE *stops by* JOHNSON) This is my manservant Birdy Johnson. I beg you not to ask him any questions. His mind is in its original state of white paper.

JOHNSON. (*Quickly*) Do you require anything, sir?

ROSS. Chairs for a start. I am afraid my general disinclination for company has turned my sitting room into a standing room.

(JOHNSON *leaves*. ROSS *spins his chair and faces* WATSON)

Are you a doctor?

WATSON. I am!

ROSS. Ignorant profession! (*Crossing to* HOLMES. *Merrily*) Mr. Holmes, they say a house is turned upside down when you enter it. Nothing but guessing and speculating, and speculating and guessing; waiters and chambermaids speculating in the kitchen, footmen and gardeners speculating in the shrubbery. Why, I have heard that in the stables of houses you visit, the very horses fall into speculative postures.

HOLMES. (*Sharply*) Clap an extinguisher on your irony, sir! Your life may be in danger.

ROSS. (*Alarmed*) What do you mean?

HOLMES. Calm yourself, Major Ross. Take a pinch of your snuff.

ROSS. How do you know I use snuff?

HOLMES. Although you are careful to remove all traces of it from your face with the handkerchief you keep up the sleeve of your dressing-gown, a true military habit, the nail of the index finger of your left hand, you are left-handed, is encrusted with a burgundy powder, which due to its unique hue, can only be the Mahareeny brand of snuff, created by the East India Company. (*During this speech* HE *has deliberately worked his way over to the door of the room, which* HE *now opens quickly.* JOHNSON *has been listening behind it*)
Come in, Mr. Johnson. Two inches of solid oak are not conducive to eavesdropping.

ROSS. At it again, Birdy? Incorrigible boy. You see, Mr. Holmes, the whole neighborhood is desperate to listen to you, even the half-witted. Light some candles, Birdy, for God's sake. Make yourself useful. It's so dark in here you can't even see a magnifying glass in front of your face.

(JOHNSON *lights the two candles on the table*)

HOLMES. You fail to amuse me.

ROSS. And you, me. You say my life is in danger. What reason can you possibly offer for such a monstrous assertion?

HOLMES. Perhaps this! (HE *holds* the center piece of the crucifer)

ROSS. Where did you get that?

HOLMES. My client, Miss St. Claire, brought it to us. She is afraid for her father.

ROSS. He does not require her fear. He has quite enough of his own.

HOLMES. Then you have seen it before.

ROSS. No.

HOLMES. I think you have!

ST. CLAIRE. Oh, heavenly God!

HOLMES. Tell me everything you know about this paper!

ROSS. I know nothing. I have never seen it. If you are so anxious for information about it, Mr. Holmes, why don't you deduce it for yourself? That is your forte after all, deduction. Or is it beyond you? Have your powers let you down?

HOLMES. They have not! Pray, do not fear for me, Major Ross, I beg you.

ROSS. Then tell me, amuse an old man. What on earth do you think it can be. Deduce, sir, deduce!

(*Thunder*)

HOLMES. (*Holding up* SMALL's *piece of the crucifer*) It is a crucifer, an ancient sign, meaning that which bears a cross. Among the Christians, it signified a sacred oath that was never written down, so that their plans would be secret. This one is unique because it is drawn in blood. A convex lens, and a strong light will further show that there are three different thumbprints, also of blood, made while handling the paper. (HE *turns it over*) The other side is a section of a regulation map of a fort with many gates. Some forty-five are shown and this is only the center. A man of education thinks immediately of the Red Fort of Agra; the only structure in the world with a hundred gates. Now, it is common knowledge that you and St. Claire served during the Mutiny. So—here is a desperate gesture, an oath in blood, in a time of revolution. But, in detection, what is out of the common is usually a guide rather than a hindrance. These bloody thumbprints, for instance, tell their own tale: Captain St. Claire fell in his hallway yesterday, leaving some bloody prints on the wall. This is his thumbprint. I believe that the second print is yours. What I want from you, Major Ross, is the following information. Who was the third man, what was the oath, and most important of all, in the event that that oath be broken, what precisely was the curse that would ensue?

ROSS. (*Astounded*) Really, Mr. Holmes, if you'd lived a hundred years ago, you would have been burned.

WATSON. Incredible!

HOLMES. (*To* ROSS) And first, before anything, I want to see your piece of it!

ROSS. (*Stunned*) Piece?

HOLMES. Please do not waste my time!

(ROSS *takes his piece of the crucifer out of his dressing gown and gives it to* HOLMES. HOLMES *places it against* SMALL's *piece which* HE *is holding. It forms two-thirds of a circle*)

Now, Captain, yours.

(ST. CLAIRE *takes his piece from the pocket of his coat and puts it against the two pieces that* HOLMES *is holding. The three pieces form a circle with a cross through the center*)

WATSON. Good heavens!

HOLMES. It is an alarming object, is it not, Watson? Now, Gentlemen, I ask you again, who was the third man?

ST. CLAIRE. His name is Jonathan Small.

ROSS. (*With cold anger—to* ST. CLAIRE) What have you done, you blithering idiot? Leave my house. Take your friends and get out of my house.

IRENE. (*Runs to* ROSS *and kneels in front of him*) Major Ross, I beg you! Help us to untangle this horror! Can we not help each other? Can we not all be friends?

(*Thunder*)

ROSS. Friends! You tell me about friends? You're too young and too silly to know. The world is nothing but a great kennel. I learned that in India in the Rajasthan Desert. We were in camp, it was July, and the heat was intolerable. I came down with a fever and was confined to my bed. There was a full moon at the time, and in consequence every dog near my tent was baying it. But the brutes assembled always in threes and fours like friends, and their conjoined sound drove me frantic. So I shot one loud-mouthed singer and suspended his carcass about fifty yards from my tent door, to frighten his friends away. But his friends fell upon, fought for, and ultimately devoured the body, and as it seemed to me, sang their hymns of thanksgiving afterward with renewed energy. It was at that moment that I understood the nature of friendship, from a pack of dogs.

(*There is a roll of thunder, this time accompanied by a long, flickering flash of lightning. The* PEDDLER *stands on the outside of the window, which is open. It is* JONATHAN SMALL)

SMALL. (*Shouting*) This dog is still alive.

ROSS. You!

SMALL. Yes, it is I. Jonathan Small. The best dog of the rich. He is not dead yet. (HE *is gone*)

ROSS. I didn't recognize him. He has a wooden stump all the way up to his thigh.

HOLMES. Quick, Watson, after him.

(WATSON *runs to the window, tries to climb out and gets stuck*)

Not that way, man, use your eyes.

(WATSON *extricates himself*)

Lock that window and follow me. (*To* JOHNSON) Mr. Johnson don't let anyone in this room. (HE *takes a candle from the table*) Hurry, Watson. (HE *runs out of the door*)

WATSON. (*Goes to* IRENE) Miss St. Claire, will you be all right?

IRENE. Yes. I am not afraid.

(WATSON *takes the remaining candle and rushes out the door which* JOHNSON *quickly closes. The room is dark; the only light comes from the window and the glowing fireplace*)

Wait! The candle!

ST. CLAIRE. Irene. Where are you?

IRENE. I'm here, Father.

ROSS. Birdy, light a candle.

JOHNSON. I have to go to the kitchen to get one. Mr. Holmes said not to open—

ROSS. Hurry up, man!

(*Lightning flashes again. The Pollard lime tree moves. A branch seems to come away and what looks like a shadow leaps onto the outside of the window and hangs like a large cross over the pane*)

ST. CLAIRE. (*Screaming*) The sending, the curse, it is here. I told you!

(*The window opens and the shadow seems to drop into the room*)

ROSS. Who's there? Birdy, is that you? (ROSS *wheels his chair into the shaft of light coming through the window. With an effort* HE *gets to his feet and raises his cane as if* HE *would strike something. Suddenly* HE *grabs his throat and cries out in pain. Choking*) You black devil. He's been watching all the time. He knows where it is. (HE *raises his cane and brings it down as if* HE *would strike someone*) You cannot have it. It is mine!!! MINE!!! (HE *cries out again and grabs the other side of his throat. This time* HE *falls to the floor.* IRENE *faints. Her body can be seen by the fireplace in its glow.* ST. CLAIRE *runs out of the room, followed by* BIRDY JOHNSON. *Suddenly,* ROSS's *body, lying in the shaft of light from the window, seems to rise up, and finally it falls on its back—feet facing the window. Pinned to his chest is a strip of paper. It is the crucifer;* ROSS's *piece.*

The stage is dark)

SCENE THREE

Part Two

The same—two hours later.

A match is struck in the darkness. It is WATSON. HE holds a candle which HE lights. IRENE sits on one of the chairs Downstage. ROSS's body lies on the floor where we saw it fall. It is covered with his lap rug. The storm is over.

IRENE. How much longer must we wait?

WATSON. Holmes has sent for Inspector Lestrade of Scotland Yard. We must give our evidence as to the details of this murder. Then we can go back to London and find your father.

IRENE. I hope we are not too late.

(HOLMES *rushes into the room followed by* INSPECTOR LESTRADE, *a small, ferretlike man with enormous energy. It is clear that* HE *feels himself in competition with* HOLMES, *who treats him with courtesy that is obviously an effort.* LESTRADE *wears a loud, three-piece plaid suit*)

HOLMES. Inspector Lestrade, this is my client, Miss St. Claire.

LESTRADE. (*Kissing her hand*) How do you do, miss? Nasty business, nasty business. We will conclude this investigation as soon as possible, and you can leave this dreary place.

IRENE. Whatever I can do, Inspector.

LESTRADE. (*Looking around the room*) That is Major Ross? (HE *indicates the body*) I hope you haven't touched anything, Holmes.

HOLMES. I am not in the habit of touching things until the police arrive, Lestrade.

LESTRADE. Good evening, Watson.

WATSON. Lestrade.

LESTRADE. Well, to work. Find your place and hold it: find

your work and do it. And put everything you've got into it. That's what I say.

(HOLMES *sighs*. LESTRADE *looks at the body, removing the lap rug*)

HOLMES. (*Crosses to* IRENE *as if to distract her from looking at the body again*) What will you do now?

IRENE. I suppose the only thing I can do is return to Camberwell and wait for my father.

HOLMES. He will not go back to Camberwell.

IRENE. No.

HOLMES. I don't think it is wise for you to go there either. I would suggest that you return with us to Baker Street for tonight.

WATSON. That's a splendid idea, Holmes. She can have my room and I'll sleep in the sitting room.

IRENE. I don't want to cause you any bother. I just want to find my father.

HOLMES. My dear. There were two horses in the stable. They are gone. Your father and Mr. Johnson have unquestionably taken them. They escaped while Watson and I were following Jonathan Small. By now they are in London, and I know that we can find them before anything else happens. Where do you think your father has gone?

IRENE: To Limehouse.

HOLMES. To an opium den?

IRENE. Yes.

HOLMES. My work has taken me to such places before, and I have one or two favors owing me in that district. Promise me you will not worry. We will leave here shortly.

IRENE. (*Smiling*) I promise.

LESTRADE. (*Concluding his examination*) I have examined the body and the room. Now, from what Holmes has told me about what went on here before this phantom appeared, I would say it is all very simple.

WATSON. Really?

LESTRADE. Yes. (HE *sits*) All this talk of revenge and curses has put you all on edge. When Small appeared at the window he frightened everyone, then the room being darkened frightened everyone some more. (*Pointing to the window*) That Pollard lime tree was your evil spirit. When the lightning struck, its shadow fell in the room. This man Ross, was ill, to judge by his wheel chair. He was finished off by terror, terror and possibly guilt. There are no marks on the body. So he obviously died of a heart seizure. As to the others; the manservant and your father ran away because they were frightened. And all because of a Pollard tree. You have been the victims of a common hallucination. (HE *smiles smugly*)

HOLMES. Well, is that it, Lestrade? Those are your conclusions?

LESTRADE. They are.

HOLMES. Let me congratulate you. You have done very well indeed. It's true you have managed to miss every detail of importance.

LESTRADE. I beg your pardon?

HOLMES. (*Crosses to him*) My dear Lestrade. You know me too well to think that I am boasting when I say that I shall destroy your theory by means of which you are quite incapable of employing, or even understanding.

LESTRADE. What means are those?

HOLMES. Intelligence and common sense. (*Crossing to* ROSS's *body*) Beginning with the victim. You have failed to notice the two very small punctures on either side of the neck.

LESTRADE. (*Defensively*) I noticed them. The man was obviously a careless shaver.

HOLMES. Fancy! (*Prying* ROSS's *hand open*) And is this his razor? (HOLMES *takes a splinter of wood from* ROSS's *hand*)

LESTRADE. What is that? It looks like a thorn.

HOLMES. It is a thorn.

(LESTRADE *reaches for it*)

Be careful, for it is unquestionably poisoned.

LESTRADE. Poisoned?

HOLMES. Precisely! The enforced administration of poison is by no means a new thing in criminal annals. The case of Dolsky in Odessa, and of Lecocque in Montpelier will occur at once to any toxicologist.

LESTRADE. What does it all mean?

HOLMES. It means murder, Lestrade. What do you think it means? Watson?

WATSON. (*Coming over to them*) Yes, Holmes?

HOLMES. Just put your hand here on this poor fellow's arm, and here on his leg. What do you feel?

WATSON. The muscles are as hard as a board. They are in a state of extreme contraction, far exceeding the usual rigor mortis.

HOLMES. Quite so. Coupled with this distortion of the face, this Hippocratic smile, or *Risus Sardonicus* as the old writers called it, what would it suggest to your mind?

WATSON. Death from some powerful vegetable alkaloid.

LESTRADE. Alkaloid?

WATSON. Some substance like strychnine which would produce tetanus.

HOLMES. Excellent, Watson, you really are invaluable. That is the idea which occurred to me the instant I saw his face. On getting into the room I at once looked for the means by which the poison had entered the system. As you saw, I discovered a thorn which had been driven or shot into the victim's neck. (*To* LESTRADE) Now examine the thorn. Is that an English thorn?

LESTRADE. I'm scarcely an expert in thorns, Holmes.

HOLMES. Quite right! Now I am going to strain your powers to

their height. After Small appeared at the window, he went to
the cab that had brought us here, instructed the driver to take
him to the station, and immediately got out on the other side
and disappeared into the trees, thereby leading Watson and me
on a merry chase.

WATSON. Then there was someone else involved?

HOLMES. Exactly, a very able and efficient ally.

LESTRADE. Ally?

HOLMES. Yes, Watson. And this is where the case assumes fea-
tures of genuine singularity. I fancy the nature of this ally
breaks fresh ground in the annals of crime in this country—
though parallel cases suggest themselves from Mozambique
and, if my memory serves me, from Senegambia.

WATSON. What do you mean?

HOLMES. To begin with. How came he into the room? Johnson
was guarding the door and the window was locked.

WATSON. Yes, I locked it myself.

LESTRADE. Did you? (*Going to the window*)

WATSON. I simply don't understand. I swear to you, Holmes, I
locked that window. I'll take my oath on it.

IRENE. But even open, the window is too small for a man to
come through.

HOLMES. (*Pleased*) Thank you, Miss St. Clair. (*Points to the
floor*) Now observe, the floor is covered with prints of a naked
foot—

LESTRADE. So it is.

HOLMES. Clear, well-defined, perfectly formed, but scarce half
the size of those of an ordinary man.

WATSON. Holmes, you mean a child has done this horrid thing?

HOLMES. No.

LESTRADE. What are you telling us?

HOLMES. My dear Lestrade, you know my methods. With all

these data you should be able to draw some just inference. Diminutive foot marks—naked feet—great agility—and poisoned darts—Well?

WATSON. A savage! An Indian who was associated with Small during the mutiny.

HOLMES. Superb, Watson. You really are on form tonight. A savage, certainly, but not, I think, an Indian. Some of the inhabitants of the Peninsula are small men, but none could have left such marks as these. The Hindu proper has long and thin feet. The sandal-wearing Mohammedan has his great toe well separated from the others to accommodate the thong commonly passed between them. These thorns too could only be shot in one way. They are from a blowpipe. Now then, Lestrade, where do we find our savage?

LESTRADE. (*Angrily*) How in hell should I know?

HOLMES. Andaman Islands, 440 miles west of Rangoon in the Bay of Bengal. Mark that, Watson. The aborigines of the Andaman Island may perhaps claim the distinction of being one of the smallest races upon this earth. They are a fierce, morose, and intractable people, though capable of forming most devoted friendships when their confidence has been gained.

IRENE. Your knowledge seems to be inexhaustible. But how did Jonathan Small come to have so singular a companion?

HOLMES. The Andaman Island is the largest British prison in India. Small has obviously been there since the mutiny, and he's made friends with a pygmy islander who undoubtedly helped him to escape from that hellhole.

WATSON. Remarkable!

HOLMES. (*Crossing to the window*) Meretricious. What we are concerned about here is motive. Our pygmy was carrying something rather heavy when he left this room.

LESTRADE. How can you possibly know that?

HOLMES. If you had read my monograph on footprints and their relation to weight, you would know the answer to that, Lestrade.

LESTRADE. I did. Found it frightfully boring.

HOLMES. (*With a withering look at* LESTRADE) The foot-prints coming up to the window are about a half inch deep. The footprints going away from the window are an inch deep. (*Going to the wheel chair*) And this chair has a hidden compartment. These things would be apparent to you, if you would use your eyes.

LESTRADE. (*Confused*) I was going to look at that chair.

HOLMES. What do you make of it?

LESTRADE. I don't know what to make of it.

HOLMES. That is because you failed at the beginning of this inquiry to grasp the importance of the most apparent clue presented to you, the crucifer. (HE *kneels by* ROSS's *body and picks up the crucifer*) Two officers in command of a fort in India, swear a sacred and secret oath of loyalty, drawn in blood with this man Small. The time, the place, the size and weight of what was concealed in the chair, leaves one to conclude that they had stolen an invaluable treasure of some kind. Small helps them to secure the treasure, and they betray him. (HE *looks at* IRENE *with concern*) Forgive me, Miss St. Claire.

IRENE. No, Mr. Holmes, now at least I know. Whatever crime my father has committed, he has paid a thousand times over.

LESTRADE. But all this is mere theory.

HOLMES. It is more than that. It is the only hypothesis which covers the facts. Let us see how it fits in with the sequel. Major Ross remains at peace for some years, happy in the possession of the treasure. St. Claire rejects it because he fears the oath in his own blood which he has broken. Then he receives a letter which gives him a terrible fright.

IRENE. A piece of the agreement that proved that the man they had wronged had been set free.

HOLMES. Or had escaped. That is much more likely. (*To* LES-TRADE) Does this reasoning strike you as faulty?

LESTRADE. No. It is clear. The case is complete.

HOLMES. Not quite. This murder could not have been committed without help from inside the house. There are two punctures in Ross's neck, but only one dart. Someone inside this house unlocked the window and retrieved the dart.

LESTRADE. The manservant, Johnson. He must be the accomplice. There's no one else.

HOLMES. You mean the butler did it! Really, Lestrade!

LESTRADE. Or St. Claire.

IRENE. Oh, God!

HOLMES. (*Sharply*) Lestrade, your methods are as subtle as those of your tailor.

LESTRADE. (*Looking at his suit*) What do you mean?

HOLMES. Never mind.

LESTRADE. Why not? St. Claire and Small could have formed an alliance to revenge themselves on Ross and recover the treasure.

IRENE. If that were true, I would never allow the treasure to remain in our family after the havoc it has caused.

HOLMES. I am happy you feel that way. The treasure belongs to the British government.

LESTRADE. (*Suddenly realizing*) But where is it?

HOLMES. Small has it.

IRENE. I would like to see it. I would like to look on that thing that has ruined the lives of everyone around me.

HOLMES. I promise you, Miss St. Claire, that once we have recovered it you shall gaze upon it to your heart's content. How are you feeling?

IRENE. I am terribly afraid for my father.

HOLMES. Then let us leave for London at once. Come along, Lestrade, we have work to do.

LESTRADE. We do?

HOLMES. I must know what happened that night at Agra. What

was the curse, should the oath be broken? Why is the crucifer placed on Ross's chest?

LESTRADE. Well, I would like to know whether Watson locked that window or not. Your whole guess about an accomplice rests on that point.

HOLMES. Dr. Watson is a sterling fellow. If he says he locked a window, he locked it. He is not a mental deficient like some members of the Metropolitan Police.

(THEY *are gone.* IRENE *starts for the door*)

WATSON. Miss St. Claire, would you stay a moment?

IRENE. What is it, Dr. Watson?

WATSON. I wish you would call me John. I want to say something to you.

IRENE. Yes?

WATSON. It's just that—don't concern yourself with the future. I hope you'll let me help you. I should be proud to be responsible for you.—Oh, God, I don't know what I'm saying—I'm all feelings. I've never met anyone like you.

IRENE. How kind you are. In these days of perfect manners, it's so refreshing to see anything like natural expression on a man's face.

WATSON. (*Hopefully*) Miss St. Claire—Irene—I want to tell you—

IRENE. Dr. Watson, it's been an amazing day. We've been hurled into each other's lives with the force of a hurricane. I don't understand any of the things I feel. I owe you and Mr. Holmes my sanity. You're a man of such delicacy. I'm sure you understand.

WATSON. Of course I do. Let us go at once. (HE *looks at* ROSS's *body*)

IRENE. (*At the door*) What is it?

WATSON. The crucifer. Holmes said it was the most important clue, yet he left it behind. (HE *picks up the crucifer*) Do you think I should take it?

IRENE. (*Looking at* ROSS) No. Put it back! That is where it belongs.

(WATSON *puts the crucifer back on* ROSS's *chest, picks up
the candle, and* THEY *leave, closing the door. The moonlight
through the window becomes more intense.* ROSS *lies in this
shaft of light, with black all around him. The crucifer lies
glowing on his breast.*

The lights fade)

Intermission

SCENE FOUR

The Gate of a Hundred Sorrows—an opium den.

The stage is dark. Music. A scream is heard. A match is struck illuminating the face of ST. CLAIRE. HE *sits on a pallet on the floor. The match is held by* FUNG TCHING, *a Chinaman, who steps upon a stool and lights an Oriental lantern, which now reveals a large room.*

Across the back, cribs on which bodies are half-visible, drugged and asleep in the shadows. On Stage Left, a stairway leading into the room. On Stage Right, a door that leads out onto the wharves. A coffin, covered wih red and gold dragons, stands in an upright position in the Center of the room. On Stage Left, a brazier burns.

FUNG TCHING *is ancient.* HE *wears a black Mandarin robe with bright embroidery and a hat.*

It is midnight of the following day, after the events at Pondicherry Lodge.

ST. CLAIRE *is drugged and frightened.*

ST. CLAIRE. Where am I?

FUNG TCHING. You are in the Gate of a Hundred Sorrows, Captain St. Claire.

ST. CLAIRE. I knew a sorrow, once, that had a hundred gates.

FUNG TCHING. How do you feel?

ST. CLAIRE. On the soul which I have lost and on the conscience which I have killed, I tell you that I cannot feel. I am as the Gods, knowing good and evil but untouched by either. Is this enviable or not?

FUNG TCHING. The Chinese say that envy is like a fly that passes all a body's sounder parts and dwells upon the sores.

ST. CLAIRE. What time is it?

FUNG TCHING. To answer your question, it has recently struck midnight. To answer your need, it is time for another pipe. (HE *crosses to the brazier and fetches a pipe*)

ST. CLAIRE. When did I come here?

FUNG TCHING. Last evening.

ST. CLAIRE. It is very hard to keep count of time in the Gate. A very long time ago, I had a wife of sorts, but she is dead now. People say that I killed her by taking the black smoke, and—

(FUNG TCHING *hands him the pipe. During the following exchange* HE *takes opium from his pocket and rolls it into a ball, preparing the pipe*)

Perhaps I did, but it is so long since, that it doesn't matter.

FUNG TCHING. I murdered my wife, so they tell me.

ST. CLAIRE. My wife was a good woman.

FUNG TCHING. There was nothing good about Madame Fung Tching. She was a very dirty hill-coolie woman, with goiter. There was a legend among the hills that she had once been young; but no living man was prepared to come forward and say boldly that the legend was true. (HE *hands* ST. CLAIRE *the prepared pipe, then crosses to the brazier to fetch a taper*) As she grew older, she showed no sign of softness, mellowness, or charm. Besides perpetual health, she had discovered the secret of perpetual bad temper. (HE *crosses back to* ST. CLAIRE *and lights the pipe*) From a mere woman, she grew to be an institution. There was no one like her, though there were many imitations. At this time, I owned a spice shop in Calcutta, and was drinking rather heavily. One night, they say, I filled her full of red pepper and hung her from a beam in the Babu Mosque. A murder in the Indian manner. Luckily, the death of an Oriental woman in an Asiatic country does not attract much attention. Nevertheless, I swore to give up drink. That is why I dropped bazaar-rum and took to the black smoke. One needs no wife if one is married to opium.

ST. CLAIRE. (*Beginning to feel the opium*) Am I dead, by any chance?

FUNG TCHING. Why do you speak of death?

ST. CLAIRE. I came here to die.

FUNG TCHING. And why is that?

ST. CLAIRE. I must join my friend, Ali. He died last night. I heard the gurgle in his throat. (HE *takes his piece of the crucifer out of his pocket*) We are partners, you see, and an angel is coming for me. A peg-legged angel.

(IRENE *stands on the stairs*. WATSON *is behind her*)

FUNG TCHING. Is this the angel who comes for you?

IRENE. Father? (*Rushing to him*) How long have you been here?

ST. CLAIRE. We must hang up a large black jar outside our window to ward off the evil eye.

IRENE. Yes. We'll do it now. Let us go to Camberwell.

ST. CLAIRE. On the soul of your mother, I swear no harm shall come to you. Whatever happens to me.

IRENE. Won't you come away with me now?

ST. CLAIRE. (*Dreaming*) I can't now. I have started a pipe. When it is finished the dragons will move about and fight.

IRENE. (*Humoring him*) Where are they?

ST. CLAIRE. (*Points at the black coffin*) There.

IRENE. (*Gasping*) What is that?

FUNG TCHING. This is my coffin. (HE *crosses to it and opens the lid. It is lined with red plush*) I brought it all the way from China with me. When I die, it will go to China again—with me, and two ounces of smoke inside it. In case I should want some on the way.

IRENE. (*Desperately—to* WATSON) What are we to do?

WATSON. I don't know. (*Angrily—to* FUNG TCHING) This filthy place should be closed, and you should be thrown in prison.

FUNG TCHING. And who are the greater criminals—those who sell the instruments of vice, or those who use them?

ST. CLAIRE. My pipe's gone out.

FUNG TCHING. (*Goes to the brazier to fetch a taper*) I will light it.

IRENE. No, please! He's half mad already.

ST. CLAIRE. A woman's corpse is coming down the hill to the burning-ghat. She died at midnight from the heat. (HE *falls over*.

IRENE *kneels beside him*. WATSON *crosses to* FUNG TCHING *at the brazier*)

WATSON. For God's sake, man, can't you help us to get this poor fellow out of here?

FUNG TCHING. (*In a different voice*) That is the last thing I will help you to do, Watson! The last! (HE *removes his hat and wig*)

WATSON. (*Dumbfounded*) Holmes!

HOLMES. Shh! (HE *looks over at* IRENE *who, tending to* ST. CLAIRE, *has seen nothing*) Keep your voice down.

WATSON. I got your message to meet you. But how do you come to be here?

HOLMES. The real Fung Tching is a friend of mine. I was some assistance to him in solving the riddle of the Peking duck poisoning at Pentonville. He was wrongfully accused. These are his clothes. Now, listen carefully. Lestrade and his police are watching the street. (*Indicating the door to the wharf*) That door leads to a wharf. There is a policeman out there. I have had word that Jonathan Small is checking all the opium houses. When he comes here, I will be waiting.

WATSON. What do you want me to do?

HOLMES. Take Miss St. Claire up to the slop house that fronts this sordid place. But don't eat anything. And do not come back here, until I send for you. I want no distractions in case anything should happen.

ST. CLAIRE. (*Crying out*) Where's my pipe?

IRENE. Dr. Watson, please look at him. His breathing is so irregular.

(WATSON *goes to* ST. CLAIRE *and kneels beside him*)

ST. CLAIRE. I'm a bit screwed, but a dip in loggerhead will put me right again.

WATSON. (*To* IRENE) Loggerhead. That's what our soldiers call the Oudh River. He thinks he's in India. (HE *takes the stethoscope out of his hat and puts it to* ST. CLAIRE's *chest*)

ST. CLAIRE. Have you spoken to Wali Dad about the pony's knees? Lend me fifty rupees.

WATSON. Now, Captain, Loggerhead is three thousand weary miles away. (*To* IRENE) It's strange to hear the old names again. (*To* ST. CLAIRE) I've served in India, too. That's where I got my game leg.

ST. CLAIRE. The summer rains are late, and maybe they come out of season. Come. (HE *stands, unsteadily*) Mrs. St. Claire has prepared supper. We shall dine on the roof, and count the stars, but only a few, for the sky is heavy with cloud. (*To* IRENE) Come, put on your richest jewels.

WATSON. (*To* Irene—*putting his stethoscope away*) He's fine.

ST. CLAIRE. And you are a gentleman. You shall share such hospitality as my poor house affords.

WATSON. Thank you.

ST. CLAIRE. Thanks—a thousand thanks. I would introduce you to my wife, were I sober—or she tolerable. (HE *falls to the floor*)

IRENE. (*Kneels by him*) Captain?

ST. CLAIRE. Yes, Major?

IRENE. It is dangerous if you remain here. You must come away.

ST. CLAIRE. (*Whispering*) Oh, no, my dear. I'm so afraid of dying in the open.

IRENE. Father, I beg you.

ST. CLAIRE. (*Roughly pushes her away*) If I can attain heaven with a pipe, why should you be envious?

WATSON. He doesn't understand.

IRENE. (*Taking his face in her hands*) Heaven? That is not what I see in your face. I see effeminacy, a submission to bondage. The spring of your will unwound like a broken clock. See yourself. In the robust period of life, reduced to imbecility and decay. I cannot bear to look at you like this. (SHE *picks up the pipe which has been lying by his side*) Here, smoke yourself to death! (SHE *rushes across the room to the stairs*)

WATSON. (*Going to her*) My dear.

IRENE. (*Crying*) I've never spoken to him like that.

WATSON. You are completely exhausted. He is safe here. I guarantee it. Holmes is with him.

IRENE. What do you mean?

WATSON. Come upstairs. Maybe I can get some tea in that filthy cafe. I'll explain everything.

(THEY *go up the stairs*. HOLMES *crosses to* ST. CLAIRE)

HOLMES. You were about to tell me the story of that piece of paper.

ST. CLAIRE. My pipe's gone out.

HOLMES. Tell me the story and I will light it.

(*A* VOICE *calls out feebly from one of the cribs. It is* BIRDY JOHNSON)

JOHNSON. Chinaman!

HOLMES. Oh, damn!

JOHNSON. Whatever your name is . . .

HOLMES. You are well, Mr. Birdy?

JOHNSON. How long have I been here?

HOLMES. You brought the Captain last evening. It is past midnight.

ST. CLAIRE. (*Dreaming*) The Persian and the Madras are terribly shaky now. They've got a boy to light their pipes for them. I always do that myself.

JOHNSON. Oh, Christ. How can I face her. How can I tell her. I must get home right away. (*Crosses to* ST. CLAIRE. HOLMES *watches carefully*) Captain, you took my last penny. I gave you my money, do you remember? Oh, why did I smoke that filth? Captain, I must get to my mother right away. What shall I do?

ST. CLAIRE. Hide her in the fort. It lies between the Copper-Smith's gully, and the pipe-stem seller's quarter, within a hundred yards, too, as the crow flies, of the mosque of Wazir Khan. I have a map. (HE *picks up the crucifer*) This is the Agra fort.

HOLMES. And what happened that night at the Agra fort?

ST. CLAIRE. (*To* HOLMES) He cursed us.

HOLMES. What was the curse?

ST. CLAIRE. He said if we betrayed him . . . (HE *breaks off as* LESTRADE *comes running down the steps into the room.* JOHNSON *hides by the coffin*)

LESTRADE. Holmes! Holmes! (HE *does not know that* HOLMES *is disguised*)

HOLMES. (*To* LESTRADE) Sh! Come to the fire and warm your hands. I will prepare a pipe for you.

LESTRADE. I don't want any of your filthy poison. Where is Mr. Sherlock Holmes? I know he came down here. Have you drugged him? I warn you, I'm thinking of getting public support to close down these dens of iniquity.

HOLMES. You have no little vices, Inspector Lestrade?

LESTRADE. You are impertinent for an Oriental. I have no little vices.

HOLMES. One big vice in a man is apt to keep out a great many smaller ones. I refer to stupidity.

LESTRADE. (*Outraged*) How dare you? And how did you know my name?

HOLMES. (*Pulling off his hat and wig*) For the love of God man, I'm trying to get St. Claire to talk.

LESTRADE. Holmes? You gave me a turn. (*Looks at him*) I say, that is ingenious. How do you—

HOLMES. (*Raging*) What do you want?

LESTRADE. The case is solved! I know who helped Small. (*Holds up a letter*) This is a statement on Birdy Johnson's mother. The woman robbed Ross and signed a confession which he gave to his solicitor, with instructions to send it to the police if anything happened to him. Isn't it clear? Blackmail. The Johnson boy must have hated him. He is the one who unlocked the window, and stole the thorn.

JOHNSON. (*Shrieking*) No. No. It's too late now, isn't it, it's too late! (HE *dashes up the stairs and out*)

LESTRADE. How long has he been here?

HOLMES. He brought the Captain here last night.

LESTRADE. Aha! He brought St. Claire here to kill him.

HOLMES. Well, we won't know that now since you frightened him away. Well, for God's sake man, are you going to let him escape?

LESTRADE. I'll get him. (HE *dashes up the stairs, on his way crashing into* WATSON *who is coming down*)

HOLMES. Watson, what is it?

WATSON. (*Desperate*) Holmes, come up to the cafe. Oh God! I think Irene's been poisoned.

HOLMES. How on earth—Never mind! Lestrade, why are you standing there? Are you going to let Johnson escape? Get him before you are too old to run.

(LESTRADE *runs up the stairs, blowing a police whistle*)

Watson, stay here and watch St. Claire. I will see to his daughter.

WATSON. But Holmes.

HOLMES. (*Sharply*) Stay here! (HOLMES *runs up the stairs. Suddenly, after all the commotion, it is very quiet*)

ST. CLAIRE. Her mother died violently; Alice.

WATSON. (*Staggers slightly*) Captain, I thought you were asleep.

ST. CLAIRE. No one will light my pipe.

(WATSON *falls to his knees by* ST. CLAIRE. HE *is behaving strangely, as if drugged*)

Why don't you go to sleep? (*Crooning to* WATSON) The moon has gone out. The dogs are very still. And the caravans go up and the caravans go down, and a hundred fires sparkle in the gut of the pass. (*Looking around him*) Now it is quiet. Now I can dream.

(WATSON *is asleep at* ST. CLAIRE's *feet. Music. The lightning becomes unreal.* ST. CLAIRE *is hallucinating. There is a thumping sound as of a wooden leg striking the floor in time with the music*)

(*Alarmed*) Small? Is that you?

ROSS. (*Whispering—a voice from nowhere*) Nelly! Nelly!

ST. CLAIRE. Ali? Come and talk to me.

(*The door of the coffin opens.* ROSS *is standing inside.* HE *is dressed in his officer's uniform, but his body and face are old*)

ROSS. Are you lonely?

ST. CLAIRE. Oh yes. I've been lonely since that night.

ROSS. Come with me.

ST. CLAIRE. (*Rises and participates in his own dream*) Where are we going?

ROSS. To the entrance. The entrance of the Old Quarter. We must stop Small as he comes out. Before he has time to hide the scroll.

(THEY *stand on either side of the black coffin. Inside it,* SMALL *appears, young and in uniform, looking as* HE *did in the prologue*)

SMALL. You were to wait for me at the gate.

ROSS. You're under arrest.

SMALL. What's the charge?

ROSS. The leper and the two Indians were all carrying money, given to them by Wazir Khan to hide the treasure. You murdered them for that money. Just over two hundred rupees. More than you earn in a year. We will put it in your pockets.

SMALL. (*Puts his hands to his pockets and sinks down as if from the weight*) I'll tell the truth about the chest.

ROSS. (*Pointing his cane, as if it were a pistol*) No you won't. Give me the scroll or I'll kill you now.

(*From behind,* SMALL *produces an hourglass which* HE *turns over and hands to* ROSS)

Thank you. Without the scroll you will not be able to find your way back through the labyrinth. There will be no evidence of a treasure. St. Claire will take the scroll and hide it. I will take you to the guardhouse.

ST. CLAIRE. No.

SMALL. Oh, God help me

ROSS. You will spend the rest of your life on the Andaman Islands.

(*The* YOUNG SMALL *stands in the coffin. Slowly, during the following exchange, the image blurs and changes to the* OLD SMALL, *with wooden leg and eye patch*)

It's so amusing. They breed strange mosquitoes in that part of the world, Small. They bite repeatedly, and always in the same place!

SMALL. (*Puts his hand over the missing eye*) Over and over again. And then it infected. Fluid ran down for months. One day the eyeball just rolled out in my hand. (HE *holds his hand out for* ST. CLAIRE *to see. The eye is in it*)

ST. CLAIRE. No, no!

ROSS. (*Greatly amused*) Tell him about your leg.

SMALL. It was torn off. In a river. I don't know how. Some water beast. A shark or crocodile.

ST. CLAIRE. (*Sobbing*) Oh, God! God! Can you ever forgive me?

SMALL. (*Quietly*) No. You have broken your oath. (HE *steps out of the coffin*)

ST. CLAIRE. Yes.

ROSS. Well, I'll leave you two alone. You must have so much to talk about after all these years.

ST. CLAIRE. Ali? What's it like to be dead?

ROSS. It is amazing to find oneself still in the swing of things. Do you realize that dead men's opinions in all things control the living truth? You believe in dead men's religion, you laugh at dead men's jokes, you cry at dead men's pathos. Everywhere and in all matters, dead men tyrannize over you. I like it! (HE *goes into the coffin*)

ST. CLAIRE. Don't go.

ROSS. I must, but when we are all cherubim together, my dear, good friend, you will head the conspiracy for plucking out Gabriel's tailfeathers or stealing Peter's keys. Then I shall report you. Good-by. Have a nice death. (HE *closes the lid of the coffin. Music stops. The lighting returns to normal. The dream is over. By the pallet, with wooden leg and eye patch, stands the real* JONATHAN SMALL)

ST. CLAIRE. Jonathan Small.

SMALL. Yes, it is I. And you know what must follow.

ST. CLAIRE. The curse.

SMALL. Yes, the curse.

ST. CLAIRE. (*Looks steadily at* SMALL, *and for the first time in the scene,* HE *seems to be sober*) It is good to see you. (*Hands him the opium pipe*) Do me the courtesy to light my pipe and then kill me.

SMALL. With pleasure, Captain. (SMALL *crosses to the brazier*)

ST. CLAIRE. I shall lie back, now, quiet and comfortable, and watch the red and gold dragons have their last big fight together.

(SMALL *crosses back to him with a burning taper*)

From the night, through the day, and into the night again I shall sleep; and be the master of my dreams.

SMALL. (*Feeding him the pipe and lighting it*) Come, a good stout puff. Puff out the very bottom of your heart, if any heart you have or any bottom to it.

ST. CLAIRE. (*Draws a large puff, and falls back gagging. HE opens his mouth, blood runs down his chin. HE hands SMALL his piece of the crucifer*) Take it! Cover me! It is over! (He *dies*)

SMALL. God have mercy on your soul.

(*From Offstage there is noise. HOLMES calling to LESTRADE. SMALL quickly leaves by the door that leads to the wharf. HOLMES comes down the stairs carrying IRENE. SHE is wide-eyed and obviously drugged. LESTRADE follows him*)

HOLMES. I have been outwitted, Lestrade, and I fear the worst.

LESTRADE. Is she all right?

HOLMES. (*Puts IRENE by ST. CLAIRE*) Drugged. I found her two streets away. Note the dilated pupils and the reduced circulation. The tea pot was still on the table, laced with a great deal of Alwa opium. A distinctly bitter taste. She will be herself in a few hours. (HE *feels* ST. CLAIRE's *wrist*) I have other and more alarming concerns. Where is Johnson?

LESTRADE. (*Embarrassed*) He got away. Fast runner that. But, not to worry, I sent all my men after him.

HOLMES. (*Alarmed*) All your men? Including the one who was watching the wharf?

LESTRADE. But surely, Watson was here.

HOLMES. If you will look over there, Lestrade, you will see that Watson is fast asleep. Drugged, I have no doubt, by that Lascar devil upstairs, with the same pot of tea.

LESTRADE. Well, no harm done. (*Looking around*) Everything seems to be in order.

(IRENE *has touched* ST. CLAIRE's *face.* SHE *sees the blood on her hand and screams*)

HOLMES. In perfect order, for the killer. (*To* LESTRADE) The drugging created a splendid diversion and allowed Small to slip in here and murder St. Claire.

LESTRADE. St. Claire is dead?

HOLMES. Use your eyes man. Is he breathing?

LESTRADE. (*Crosses to* ST. CLAIRE *and examines him*) This is awkward, Holmes. Right under our noses, as it were.

HOLMES. I have never been so fiendishly tricked.

WATSON. (*Awake*) Holmes, what happened?

HOLMES. (*Crossing to him*) Are you rational, man?

WATSON. I think so. (*Looking at* ST. CLAIRE) Oh, my God, I fell asleep.

HOLMES. I told you not to eat anything. How much of that tea did you drink?

WATSON. Tea. In the cafe? Only a little—you mean? Irene had two cups.

HOLMES. Someone bribed that Lascar brute to put opium pills in the tea pot.

WATSON. Irene! (HE *rushes to her*)

HOLMES. She will be all right. An unpleasant experience for a young girl, but by no means fatal. (*Cross to* LESTRADE *who has finished examining* ST. CLAIRE's *body*) Well?

LESTRADE. You are wrong, Holmes. There are no signs of violence. And no prick marks either. This man was not murdered. (*He pulls back the pallet covering* ST. CLAIRE. *His piece of the crucifer lies on his chest*) Look at this!

HOLMES. Again! What does it mean? Why were these men tyrannized by scraps of paper?

LESTRADE. I don't know. But this man, anyway, died naturally.

HOLMES. Rubbish! (*Calling*) Watson!

WATSON. (*Crosses to them, and examines* ST. CLAIRE) The same symptoms as Major Ross!

HOLMES. (*Looks into* ST. CLAIRE's *mouth and removes something*) Another thorn. This one placed in the stem of his pipe. Opium that is half smoked is thick and sticky. One would have to draw quite hard on the stem to inhale the smoke. That drew the thorn into the mouth. These things are so deadly they have only to break the skin in order to prove fatal. Devilishly clever!

WATSON. Holmes, how can you forgive me? You left me in care of the Captain, and I fell asleep.

HOLMES. I never reach your limits, Watson. There are unexplored possibilities about you. Give you a drug which sends most people into trances of sensual pleasure, and you merely fall asleep.

WATSON. Please, Holmes.

HOLMES. It's not your fault. That is opium. For some, sweet dreams. For others,

(IRENE *screams and runs past them, throwing herself down at the edge of the stage*)

HOLMES. (HE *heads for the stairs*) There's not a moment to lose.

LESTRADE. Where are we going?

HOLMES. May I remind you, Lestrade, that Small has finished his work?

LESTRADE. My God, the treasure.

HOLMES. Exactly. If we are to catch him, we must leave at once.

LESTRADE. But where is he?

HOLMES. On a boat. I can't take the time now, I will explain on the way. Watson, bring Miss St. Claire upstairs. We will find a policeman to take her to Baker Street. Data, data, I cannot make bricks without clay.

(HOLMES *and* LESTRADE *are on the stairs*)

LESTRADE. What do you mean?

HOLMES. The curse, Lestrade? What was the precise phrasing of that curse?

(LESTRADE *and* HOLMES *are gone.* IRENE *lies on the floor.* WATSON *goes to her.* SHE *sits up. Music plays.* SHE *dreams*)

IRENE. Father? Father?

WATSON. (*Trying to humor her*) I am here.

IRENE. You must advise me.

WATSON. Gladly.

IRENE. I think I am in love.

WATSON. (*Looks around almost to see if anyone can hear*) What! While I have been away?

IRENE. Even so. (SHE *dreams happily*)

WATSON. The plunge must have been very sudden.

IRENE. It was. Over head and ears. As deep as a well.

WATSON. (*Mustering courage*) And why do you love him?

IRENE. He is rare. And so kind. Kindness. What a strange word to find on anybody's lips these days. It is like a style in clothes which is no longer worn. What can one do with such a word?

WATSON. It has a way of returning every now and then, when one least expects it.

IRENE. The Military bands stop a moment for breath, the hunters pause to sleep . . . and there is kindness again, nestling stubbornly in people's hearts, ready for the millennium.

WATSON. What is his name?

IRENE. His name? His name is John. (SHE *looks at him*) John.

WATSON. Oh, my dear. (HE *kisses her mouth, gently picks her up and carries her into the dark*)

SCENE FIVE

On the River Thames. Inky blackness. A foghorn croaks. Fog hangs like a curtain over everything. A small steamer glides slowly out onto the stage. Only a lantern illuminates the faces of WATSON, LESTRADE, *and* HOLMES, *who sit in the front. A* POLICEMAN, *at the back, steers the boat.*

LESTRADE. I can't see anything in this. It's a real pea soup.

HOLMES. Keep your voice down, Lestrade. Surprise is our chief weapon. We can be grateful for Her Majesty's Jubilee. The vessels are all anchored, waiting for clearance to get out of the harbor.

WATSON. How did you reach the conclusion that he was on a boat?

HOLMES. I reached this one by sitting on five pillows and consuming an ounce of shag.

LESTRADE. I hope a wild goose may not prove to be the end of our chase.

HOLMES. I think not. A one-legged man would prefer the sea to any other form of travel. His companion, however frocked he might be, would attract attention in any public conveyance. Pygmies are singular in London. A boat is the only solution.

LESTRADE. But how could you possibly know which harbor he went to?

HOLMES. While the real Fung Tching was watching St. Claire, I went to Gravesend. That is the most sordid of our ports. Few questions are asked at Gravesend. And, as there is no honor among thieves, a pound note will buy all the information you want. People tend to remember a one-legged man, traveling with a pygmy. They are on a steamer called the *Gloria Scott.*

LESTRADE. Those are not the methods I would have used.

HOLMES. I would be delighted to hear them.

LESTRADE. Well, in the first place . . .

HOLMES. But not now! Keep a sharp eye out if you please, the *Gloria Scott* lies hard to port.

(*From the back of the stage a lantern glows. The prow of a large sailing ship appears. TONGA, a black pygmy, scuttles back and forth, screaming and pointing at the MEN in the steamer. HE wears a frock coat and cape. SMALL comes out onto the prow. HE carries the chest. Putting it down, HE leans over the rail of the ship. TONGA climbs up to the mast*)

SMALL. (*Shouting*) Keep off! Keep off!! Leave me, you brute white beasts. Years and years ago, I groped into your hearts and found nothing there for my purpose. Get you gone! Keep away, until I have finished my life's work. (*HE lifts the chest onto the rail of the ship. The MEN IN THE BOAT rise and attempt to climb onto the steamer. TONGA takes out his blowpipe and puts it to his mouth. A dart sticks to the side of the boat. LESTRADE takes out his pistol and fires. TONGA falls, clinging to the mast over SMALL's head. He groans in pain and then drops to SMALL's feet*)

Ah. No. (*HE looks at LESTRADE*) Go ahead and fire. Life is nothing to me. Only let me throw this hated poison to the sea. Only the sea will take it. And so ends the story. (*SMALL hurls the chest over the side and runs to TONGA. WATSON catches the chest and puts it on the floor of the steamer. The THREE MEN scramble up the ladder onto the steamship*)

LESTRADE. Jonathan Small, I arrest you for the willful murder of Alister Ross and Neville St. Claire.

SMALL. (*HE stands by TONGA's body, holding his coat closed over his chest*) Yes. Their death lies on my soul. (*He takes WATSON's hand*) For heaven's sake, answer me a single question.

WATSON. Of course.

SMALL. Is it drowned? Is the chest in the sea?

HOLMES. (*Quickly crossing to SMALL*) Yes, it is.

SMALL. Who are you?

HOLMES. I am Sherlock Holmes.

SMALL. (*Smiling*) Ah. You're the clever one. (*Looking at* LES-TRADE) I knew it wasn't him. You led me a merry chase, Mr. Holmes.

HOLMES. And may I return the compliment, Mr. Small. Some of your maneuvers were quite beyond me.

(SMALL *gasps and falls to the deck.* WATSON *supports him*)

Would you answer one or two questions?

SMALL. Yes, I should like to leave some account of the business behind me. I don't want to be remembered as a common cut-throat.

HOLMES. Who was your accomplice?

SMALL. Tonga.

HOLMES. The pygmy?

SMALL. He helped me escape from the prison. And good he was, the crafty little devil. I couldn't kill Ross, until I knew where the treasure was. Tonga sat in the tree all day and watched until he found out. Then I got you gentlemen out of the room, and he killed Ross.

HOLMES. Who was your accomplice inside the house? Who did you bribe, to open the window and retrieve the dart?

SMALL. No one. We didn't retrieve the darts. We had plenty of them.

LESTRADE. I suppose you'll be saying next, that you always in-tended to throw the treasure into the sea.

SMALL. Not at first. But when I saw those men, Ross and St. Claire, I knew I had come out on top. The treasure did that to them. And the fear of the curse.

HOLMES. What was the curse?

SMALL. That they would die by my hand. That each man's piece of the oath should lie on his own dead breast. They were tomb-stones.

HOLMES. So that is why you put St. Claire's piece on his body.

SMALL. But I didn't.

HOLMES. You didn't?

SMALL. No, he just looked at me, and then he died.

WATSON. You didn't put one of the thorns in his pipe?

SMALL. I don't know what you're talking about. (SMALL *staggers and falls back. His coat opens. In his hand is the Kris. His chest is covered with blood*)

WATSON. Good God, man, what have you done?

SMALL. What more have I to seek? He's the only thing I ever found to companion me. A shrunken Fuzzy-Wuzzy with not two words of my own lingo. Didn't he look fine in his new frock coat? We both laughed when he put it on. And now he's gone. What more have I to achieve? I was a good man when I was young. From our youth we try for good, but always we are lured away by phantoms—love—fame—money—one meteor of many names that vanishes in the smoke of death. My task is done, and well done. (*To HOLMES*) Where's my piece of the crucifer? Do you have it about you?

HOLMES. I do.

SMALL. Put it on my chest, Mr. Holmes. Let me die under it as the others did. A trinity of stupid men.

(HOLMES *takes* SMALL's *piece out of his pocket. He has carried it since Scene Two*)

There it is . . . The bloody sign for greed. Let me die under it and be forgotten.

(HOLMES *places the crucifer on* SMALL's *chest*)

I thank you, Mr. Holmes. (HE *dies, staring at the sky.* WATSON *closes his eyes*)

LESTRADE. Watson, can I have your handkerchief? (HE *is crying*) God help us! Why does fate play such tricks with poor helpless worms. (*To HOLMES*) He told you what you wanted to know. God keep his soul.

HOLMES. Yes.

LESTRADE. Of course, it was all lies.

HOLMES. He told me everything he knew. But there's something more.

(*The boat sails into black*)

SCENE SIX

Baker Street.

A taper glows in the dark. It is lowered to light a fireplace on Stage Left. As the fire glows, we can see IRENE, *wearing a dressing gown, leaning over the fire. It is late. Four in the morning on the same night. Irene has recovered from the opium. There is a knock at the door, Stage Right.* IRENE *crosses to the door and opens it.* JOHNSON *stands in the doorway.*

IRENE. (*Alarmed*) Mr. Johnson!

JOHNSON. (*Looks at her coldly*) Yes, miss. Is Mr. Holmes here?

IRENE. No, there's no one here. I mean they will return soon.

JOHNSON. It's just as well. You're the one I want to talk to, miss.

IRENE. About what?

JOHNSON. I want you to help me.

IRENE. How?

JOHNSON. Not in here, miss. The police may come. They're looking for me, you know.

IRENE. Yes, but what do you want of me?

JOHNSON. Are there other rooms where we might talk?

(SHE *makes a run for the door, but* HE *catches her and hurls her against the fireplace.* HE *opens the door—Left—to the bedrooms*)

This will do.

(SHE *pulls the dagger that holds* HOLMES's *letters out of the mantel of the fireplace and conceals it behind her*)

In here! (*Roughly,* JOHNSON *pushes her through the door and closes it. We hear a scream, the lights come up in the room.*

The correspondence that was fixed to the fireplace with a dagger in the second Scene is now on the floor. HOLMES,

WATSON *and* LESTRADE *walk into the sitting room.* LES-TRADE *carries the chest of jewels which* HE *puts on the floor in the Center of the room*)

LESTRADE. Well, we have only to arrest Birdy Johnson and the case is complete.

(HOLMES *throws himself onto the chaise*)

Holmes, you haven't said a word for over an hour. I said the case is complete.

HOLMES. Is it?

LESTRADE. Isn't it obvious?

HOLMES. It strikes me, my good Lestrade, as being just a trifle too obvious.

WATSON. Excuse me, gentlemen, I'm going to look in on Miss St. Claire.

HOLMES. She is probably still asleep.

(WATSON *goes through the door to the bedrooms*)

LESTRADE. Look at the facts, Holmes. Johnson is present at the time of both murders. He opens the window at the lodge, thereby aiding the pygmy. He lures the police away from the opium house, thereby aiding Small.

HOLMES. (*Sharply*) For what reason?

LESTRADE. For money. To get his mother out of the country. But we apprehend Small before he can pay Johnson off.

HOLMES. I don't mean to deny that the evidence is very strongly in favor of your theory.

LESTRADE. Well, Mr. Holmes, are you about to prove me wrong?

HOLMES. I have formed no conclusion whatsoever.

LESTRADE. But I formed mine yesterday, and now it proves to be correct. So you must acknowledge that I have been a little in front of you this time. (HE *makes to laugh—it comes out like a cackle.* WATSON *returns to the sitting room*)

WATSON. What was that noise?

HOLMES. That was Lestrade's little cock-a-doodle of victory. How is Miss St. Claire?

WATSON. I peeped through the door. She is asleep. I must say, I'm awfully jumpy. That poor man has put me completely on edge!

HOLMES. (*Quickly*) Small! Why is that?

WATSON. I felt he was telling the truth.

HOLMES. Mmm. Did you?

LESTRADE. I am a practical man, Mr. Holmes. When I have got my evidence I come to my conclusions. I find it hard enough to tackle facts without flying away after theories and fancies.

HOLMES. You are right.

LESTRADE. I am?

HOLMES. Yes. You do find it very hard to tackle facts.

LESTRADE. Oh.

HOLMES. (*Jumping up and pacing*) Yes! Yes! All the evidence points to the same conclusion. And yet—and yet—I know it is all wrong. (*Standing by the fireplace,* HE *picks up the letters which fell to the floor, and looks at them distractedly*) I feel it in my bones. However, there's no good talking about it, Watson; but unless some lucky chance comes our way, I fear that the Case of the Bloody Crucifer will not figure in that Chronicle of our success which I foresee that a patient public will sooner or later have to endure.

WATSON. You can hardly find a flaw in the case against Johnson. All further investigation has served to strengthen it.

LESTRADE. The case is as plain as a Pikestaff.

HOLMES. If you discount everything that Small said. (HE *puts his letters on the mantel*)

LESTRADE. Not quite. He did say that he didn't want to be remembered as a cutthroat. And that's why he lied.

HOLMES. Well, let us not leave the poor man's body in the

police wagon. They will be waiting for our statements at Bow Street. (HE *starts for the door*)

LESTRADE. What about the chest?

HOLMES. I promised Miss St. Claire that she could see it.

LESTRADE. Well, I suppose it will be safe here, for tonight. In the home of the great detective. Ha, ha. But Watson had better stay here with it, just in case.

WATSON. I would like to be here when Miss St. Claire wakens, in any event. She doesn't know that her father is dead.

HOLMES. (*At the door*) That is a task I do not envy, Watson. Come along, Lestrade, let's get this over with.

LESTRADE. (*Going*) Watson, please offer that charming young lady my condolences.

WATSON. Yes.

(THEY *leave.* WATSON *looks at the chest. He goes over to it, about to open it, then changes his mind*)

No, I will wait for her.

(*The door to the bedroom suddenly swings open.* IRENE *stands in it, wearing a beautiful, low-cut evening dress of red velvet*)

Irene! You are magnificent!

IRENE. Thank you, John. This gown was my mother's. I've been saving it for a special occasion.

WATSON. Special occasion?

IRENE. (*Pointing to the chest*) It is here.

WATSON. Irene, are you quite yourself? The opium—

IRENE. I am quite myself, John. (*Indicating the chest*) Open it.

WATSON. I must tell you about—Captain St. Claire.

IRENE. Open the chest, first.

WATSON. Yes, why not. Let us be carefree for the moment. We have all seen enough horror this long night.

(*The chest no longer has a lock.* HE *opens the lid. Again a glow emanates from inside*)

IRENE. Spill it out onto the floor. I want to see it flung about.

WATSON. Irene, are you certain you are feeling well?

IRENE. John, the effects of the drug have long worn off.

WATSON. Oh—very well. (HE *lifts the bottom of the chest and the jewels spill all over the floor in a great heap. This is the first time we have seen them.* IRENE *and* WATSON *both stare, transfixed.* WATSON *picks up a diamond*) It is a bonny thing! Just see how it glints and sparkles against the light. Of course, it is the nucleus and focus of crime. Every good stone is. They are the devil's pet baits.

IRENE. (*Sharply*) Put it down!

(HE *does. She walks over to the mantel of the fireplace.* WATSON *is uneasy*)

WATSON. What is the special occasion?

(SHE *is silent*)

You said you were saving the dress—for what occasion?

IRENE. A dream come true.

WATSON. My dear, it's not right. I must tell you now. Your father is dead.

IRENE. Yes. That is the special occasion.

WATSON. You don't know what you are saying. Perhaps you should lie down—

IRENE. (*Facing away from him, at the mantel*) You think I'm going mad? Too many shocks for a young lady? Oh John, the moment I walked through the door and looked into your eyes, I knew I could do it.

WATSON. (*Growing alarmed*) Do what?

IRENE. Persuade you and Mr. Holmes to help me get what is, if not legally, then rightfully mine.

WATSON. (HE *looks at the jewels*) Am I dreaming?

IRENE. If you are, this will wake you. (SHE *turns and faces him. In her hand the pistol which* WATSON *put on the mantel in Scene Two*) I opened the window at Pondicherry Lodge. I took the other thorn out of Major Ross's neck and put it into my father's pipe. My hand was trembling so that I thought I would surely pierce my own skin and die. But it didn't matter. By then, I was on fire. I felt that nothing in the world could stop me. And now, I am going to kill you, and take what I have won.

WATSON. (*Rousing himself*) Why you miserable wretch!!

IRENE. Miserable? You think it misery to be able to control the mighty, to trick a great detective—misery, to be as terrible as one is beautiful? Oh yes. You would have preferred the condition of a weak woman, exposed to all evil and capable of none.

WATSON. How can you hope to succeed? You think that Holmes will find my body and not realize what happened? You will be the most hounded criminal in Europe!

IRENE. I think not. Birdy Johnson was kind enough to call before you and Holmes returned. I took the liberty of killing him. He was under your bed, when you looked in to see if I was all right. When the police come, this is the way it will appear. Johnson came here, to collect his share of the treasure. There was a struggle, you stabbed him, he shot you. Someone heard the shot and came to find a chest full of jewels. Naturally, they took it. (SHE *laughs*) Every policeman on the force will be under suspicion. What happened to the young woman? She vanished into the fog, driven mad by the death of her father, and the more terrible death of her lover.

WATSON. You are a horror!

IRENE. And you are a darling. You were my biggest ally. Thanks, chiefly to your gullibility, I have done it.

WATSON. Yes, you poisonous thing! You have done it! And with my assistance. You have made me as hateful a creature as yourself! Now, if our breath is as fatal to ourselves as to others, let us join our lips in one kiss of unspeakable hatred, and so die!

(HE *reaches out to her.* SHE *fires the pistol.* HE *falls in front of the fireplace.* SHE *moves quickly now. Going through the door that leads to the bedrooms* SHE *returns with the dagger which* SHE *places by* WATSON's *hand.* SHE *reaches into* WATSON's *pocket and takes several pound notes which she stuffs into the bodice of her dress.* SHE *runs to the chest, puts the pistol on the floor, and begins to put the jewels back into the chest. The door to the outside opens slowly.* HOLMES *stands in it.* SHE *picks up the pistol and points it at him*)

IRENE. Come in, Mr. Holmes.

(HE *freezes*)

Are you alone?

HOLMES. Yes. I sent Lestrade ahead with the body.

IRENE. Whose body?

HOLMES. Small's.

IRENE. Small is dead? I must say, fate seems to be smiling on me for a change. Why did you come back? I am curious.

HOLMES. My dagger. (HE *indicates the mantel*) You moved my dagger from the mantel.

IRENE. I needed it. Johnson saw me open the window at Pondicherry Lodge.

HOLMES. So you have killed poor Johnson. And Watson as well.

IRENE. Johnson was too stupid to live. He would never have survived. You do not seem very concerned about Watson.

HOLMES. I am too awed by you. I cannot think of anything else.

IRENE. (*Smiling*) I have done rather well, haven't I?

HOLMES. So well that I do not understand it all.

IRENE. I thought you were omniscient, Mr. Holmes. But tell me; surely my moving the dagger was not the thing that gave me away.

HOLMES. No. It was merely the catalyst. It started a new train of thought. You see, Miss St. Claire, when you have eliminated the impossible, whatever remains, however improbable, must be the truth. You were in the room when Ross was murdered. But you were the only one who could have killed St. Claire, if Small was telling the truth.

IRENE. You could have saved my father. I put that thorn in the pipe right under your nose. But you were busy showing your Chinese costume to Watson.

(HOLMES *is stunned*)

What was my mistake?

HOLMES. The crucifer. You should not have put it on your father's body. Small felt responsible for your father's death. But he did not put the paper on his body.

IRENE. The crucifer. Well, no one is perfect.

HOLMES. You were close to perfect, Miss St. Claire. How did you manage the opium? I tasted the remains in the teapot, and I examined you. You were drugged. How could you play that pathetic scene in the opium house so securely, with opium in your body.

IRENE. There have been opium pills in our house since I was fifteen, Mr. Holmes. I discovered, a long time since, that opium could be an excellent diversion, against the long, long nights in Camberwell. I am virtually inured to it.

HOLMES. That is so grotesque that, I admit it, it never entered my mind.

IRENE. Grotesque? For a young girl to use opium? But perfectly acceptable, for the great detective to use cocaine.

HOLMES. (*Controlling his anger*) Why did you come to me in the first place?

IRENE. When the crucifer arrived in the post two days ago, my father told me the whole story. That was the first time I knew that a million in jewels had been entrusted to the care of three madmen. I could not compete with them, so I came to the great consulting detective. I thought, let him find the treasure for me, while I assist, in every way I can, to effect the curse. I depended on two facts. That you wouldn't suspect your own client, and that you would never believe a proper young woman to be capable of such atrocity. I was right on both counts. Now it is over, and there is only one man standing between me and the treasure. You, yourself. And I have a pistol.

HOLMES. Fire it, go on Miss St. Claire, I pray you. Fire that pistol.

(SHE *fires at* HOLMES. HE *doesn't move.* SHE *runs toward the door but* HOLMES *is there before her.* HE *holds her and takes the gun*)

You have made another mistake. That is Watson's starting pistol. He officiates at races and such. It is filled with blank cartridges.

IRENE. (*She looks at Watson*) But . . .

HOLMES. He fainted. Perfectly understandable, under the circumstances. Up, old boy, up.

WATSON. (HE *stands, unsteadily, looking at* IRENE) That shot, oh, God. I'm all right, Holmes. Just let me catch my breath. (HE *turns away and sinks into the chair.* HOLMES *and* IRENE *stare at each other*)

IRENE. Well, Mr. Holmes, I congratulate you.

HOLMES. Lestrade will be here in a few minutes, Watson. Then she will be gone.

IRENE. Is the prisoner allowed one last request, Mr. Holmes?

HOLMES. What is it?

IRENE. (SHE *walks down to the spilled jewels and stands over them*) Let me wear something. Just until the Inspector arrives.

HOLMES. Why not? (HE *takes an opulent ruby bracelet from the pile of jewels, and taking her hands,* HE *clasps the bracelet over her wrists and fastens it, leaving her manacled*)

IRENE. Thank you, Mr. Holmes. I am content.

(WATSON *sobs and puts his head in his hands*)

HOLMES. (*Looking at* WATSON) You are an unnatural creature, Miss St. Claire.

IRENE. Revenge is a law of human nature.

HOLMES. Revenge? Upon your own father?

IRENE. He destroyed my mother.

HOLMES. (*Coldly*) With a pistol, a dagger, a thorn?

IRENE. With syphilis.

(THEY *both look at her*)

Ah, the power, the absolute power of that word! Syphilis, the gift of an English or Indian whore. Charming, isn't it? She brought him her love and her fortune, and he, by variety life, had become diseased and thought to rid himself of it, by bringing it to her. (*Becoming quietly engrossed in her story*) He made a torture room of her body. The wheel, the rack, a bed of nails—what are these to the last stages of that disease! Nature herself is the tormentor. Nature at last casts down the wretch, searches every vein, makes a rod of every nerve, and for the scorching feet, a pain to travel on, It builds fires in the brain, and casts living coals of torment on the heart. So, before her eyes were eaten out, her nose rotted away, her skull decayed, so as to expose the brain to the size of a man's fist—she threw herself under the wheels of a train. Am I unnatural, gentlemen?

(LESTRADE *is at the door*)

Inspector Lestrade. Thank goodness. Comic relief.

LESTRADE. (*Looking at* IRENE's *manacled hands*) Then it is true. I wouldn't have believed it. How did you . . . ? (*To* HOLMES) Never mind, you can tell me the details later. Well, all's well that ends well. I mean, we have the jewels, we have her . . . and we have this. (HE *produces a letter from his pocket*) From Buckingham Palace. (HE *hands the letter to* HOLMES)

HOLMES. (*Reading*) "Her Majesty, Queen Victoria, Empress of India, will receive Inspector Lestrade at ten A.M. tomorrow, to tender him her personal thanks and to receive from his hands the great treasure of Agra."

LESTRADE. I will, of course, tell Her Majesty of your assistance, Holmes.

HOLMES. Congratulations, Lestrade.

LESTRADE. (HE *calls through the open door*) Hopkins!

(*A tall* POLICEMAN *enters the room*)

Put those jewels in that chest.

HOPKINS. (*Looking at the jewels*) Blimey!

LESTRADE. Keep your opinions to yourself. (*To* IRENE) Come along, young lady.

IRENE. There is a dead body in the next room, Birdy Johnson.

(LESTRADE *looks at* HOLMES. HOLMES *nods.* LESTRADE *signals to* HOPKINS. HOPKINS *goes into the bedroom*)

LESTRADE. (*Acutely confused*) Holmes? What shall I put in my report?

IRENE. (*Crossing down to him*) Put this. A young woman inherits a family graveyard, that being all that remains of rich hereditary possessions.

HOLMES. Write that this woman, had been nourished with poisons from her birth upward, until her whole nature was so imbued with them that she herself had become the deadliest poison in existence. Poison was her element of life. Her love would have been poison—her embrace, death. Thus, men, by their own selfishness, unwittingly fashion a creature to rule over them.

IRENE. Why, Mr. Holmes. You do understand.

LESTRADE. I can't remember all that.

IRENE. (*With great charm*) I will repeat it to you in the police wagon, Inspector. You can make notes.

(HOPKINS *comes through the bedroom door carrying* JOHNSON's *body.* HE *exits through the front door*)

LESTRADE. Yes, thank you. (HE *picks up the chest of jewels*)

IRENE. (SHE *crosses to the door*) And when you see the Queen tomorrow, tell the old girl to be careful.

LESTRADE. How's that?

IRENE. It has already destroyed everyone who has touched it, since the leper first carried it into Agra.

LESTRADE. And you think it might possibly destroy Her Majesty and perhaps the entire British Empire?

IRENE. Give it to her and see.

(SHE *throws a dazzling smile at* HOLMES *and* WATSON *and exits.* LESTRADE *follows her in a daze.* HOLMES *and* WATSON *are alone*)

HOLMES. (*Closing the door*) You will file this case away in our archives, Watson. Some day, perhaps, the true story can be told. (HE *moves Down to* WATSON) My dear old friend, there is nothing more to be said or done. You have the heartache, I have the cocaine bottle, and Lestrade has the credit. So fetch my violin and let us try to forget for half an hour, the miserable weather, and the still more miserable ways of our fellow men. (HE *puts his hand on* WATSON's *shoulder.* WATSON *moves away*)

WATSON. Thank heaven, the night is gone, at last! And I doubt whether I will spend another at Baker Street.

(HOLMES *is stunned. There is a tap at the door*)

HOLMES. What on earth? At this hour? (*Calling*) Come in!

(*A small* MAN *puts his head in the door. This is* MORDECAI SMITH, *a timid, nervous sailor*)

SMITH. Excuse me, I know it is no time to call, but I saw all the people leaving so I knew you were awake. My name is Mordecai Smith from Mobile Bay, Alabama. Are you Sherlock Holmes?

HOLMES. I am. And this is my best friend and colleague, Dr. Watson.

WATSON. If you will excuse me . . .

HOLMES. Watson, please don't go. I would be lost without my Boswell . . . (*Looking at* WATSON) You must be tired, Mr. Smith, for I perceive you have only arrived this morning from the Island of Sumatra.

SMITH. That's right . . . I docked just now on my ship the *Aurora,* but how in thunder did you know that?

HOLMES. No matter. What is your story? You are clearly terrified.

SMITH. Terrified yes, Mr. Holmes, but not drunk. Not out of my mind. (HE *falls on the table*)

HOLMES. Compose yourself, Mr. Smith. Take a chair.

(SMITH *falls into a chair*)

SMITH. Mr. Holmes, would you think me mad if I told you I'd seen a giant rat? A rat as big as a rowboat?

(WATSON *turns to look at* SMITH. HOLMES *keeps his eyes on* WATSON *who slowly comes back into the room*)

It came out of a crate on the forward deck.

HOLMES. (*Striking a match to light his pipe*) Did you see the entire animal?

SMITH. I surely did. It sprang out in one great leap, galloped down the gangplank, and disappeared into the slums. I tell you, Mr. Holmes, I've never been so frightened in my life. It's here now, in this city! It has huge mean red eyes, a rat's fangs, only gigantic. And what is worse than everything, it had in its mouth . . . (HE *faints*. WATSON *sits on the chaise transfixed*)

HOLMES. Would you be good enough to revive our client, Doctor Watson? The game is afoot! (HE *blows out the match*)

Blackout